THE FIVE MINUTE FOREMAN

THE FIVE MINUTE FOREMAN

MASTERING THE PEOPLE SIDE OF CONSTRUCTION

Mark Breslin

McAlly International Press
ALAMO, CALIFORNIA

© 2013 Mark Breslin. Printed and bound in the United States of America. All rights reserved. No part of this book may be reproduced or transmitted in any form or by any means, electronic or mechanical, including photocopying, recording, or by an information storage and retrieval system—except by a reviewer who may quote brief passages in a review to be printed in a magazine, newspaper, or on the Web—without permission in writing from the publisher. For information, please contact McAlly International Press, 1471 Livorna Road, Alamo, California, 94507.

Although the author and publisher have made every effort to ensure the accuracy and completeness of information contained in this book, we assume no responsibility for errors, inaccuracies, omissions, or any inconsistency herein. Any slighting of people, places, or organizations is unintentional.

14th printing 2023
ISBN 978-0-9741662-9-2
LCCN 2012954345

ATTENTION, UNIONS, TRAINING SCHOOLS, CONTRACTORS, UNIVERSITIES, COLLEGES, AND PROFESSIONAL ORGANIZATIONS: Quantity discounts are available on bulk purchases of this book for educational purposes, gift purposes, or as premiums for increasing magazine subscriptions or renewals. Special books or book excerpts can also be created to fit specific needs. For information, please contact McAlly International Press, 1471 Livorna Road, Alamo, California, 94507; 925-705-7662; or jdixon@breslin.biz.

www.breslin.biz

WANTED: CONSTRUCTION FOREMEN

Seeking talented individuals to run the entire construction industry.

Work long hours with little or no praise or consideration. Be willing to take on everyone's headaches including workers, subcontractors, inspectors, vendors, clients, office geeks, and anyone else who doesn't have someone to blame. Make thousands of independent decisions with an expectation of all of them being right. No professional management training provided. No professional leadership training provided. Responsible for managing tens to hundreds of millions of dollars' worth of work in your career, more or less by yourself. Figure it out as you do it. If you lose money, you will be fired. If the estimator has a lame estimate, it is still up to you to make money. No complaining allowed. Crew leadership may include but is not limited to serving as motivator, coach, therapist, teacher, mentor, trainer, mediator, and/or bail bondsman. Work with competitive, difficult, testosterone-driven Alpha males who think they are better than you. A few really smart women add sanity. Need to be ambitious, driven, focused, organized, and a little crazy. No specific qualifications. You will be thrown to the wolves. Eat or be eaten. Fun work environment. Ability to grow as a person. Discover your inner a-hole. No cubicle. Build amazing projects. Feel the pride of major industry leadership. Competitive salary and benefits.

DON'T MISS THIS GREAT OPPORTUNITY.

Table of Contents

Introduction 15

   What's in It for You: More or Less?
   Killer Tools for Your Toolbox
   Discipline, Determination, and Room to Grow
   Five Minutes a Day = 21 Hours a Year
   Five Minute Obstacles

CHAPTER 1
The Ten Faces of the Fearless Foreman 27

  1. The Bad Ass with Purpose
  2. The Protector of Life and Death
  3. The Big Money, Big Responsibility Leader
  4. The "Sink or Swim" Graduate
  5. The Moneymaking Machine
  6. The Cocky SOB
  7. The Compassionate Giver
  8. The Enforcer
  9. The Winning Coach
 10. The Role Model

CHAPTER 2

Professionalism, Safety, Integrity, and Quality 43

On Professionalism
  Blue Collar Businessperson
    Five Minutes—Owning Your Title: Professional
  The Contractor-Foreman Partnership
  The Professional: Mastering the People Side
  Ten Affirmations for the Pro Foreman
  The Pro Presentation: What the Customer Sees and Hears
  Presenting Yourself as a Leader
    Five Minutes—Auditing Your Pro Leader Image
  Understanding the Construction Business Model

On Safety
    Five Minutes—Five Safety Minutes with the New Guy
    Five Minutes—Safety Leadership: Making Consequences Real

On Integrity
  Integrity, Honesty, and Visible Values
  Accepting Responsibility (and Blame)
  Treat People Fairly

On Quality
  Schedule, Quality, and Rework
    Five Minutes—Explaining the Cost of Rework
    Five Minutes—Fixing System Failures to Improve Quality or Productivity
  Focus on the Customer
  Concentrating on What's Important
    Five Minutes—Setting Clear Expectations

Open Minds Drive Innovation
Connecting Paperwork and Profit
Five Tips for Documentation
> *Five Minutes—Organizing for Effectiveness*

CHAPTER 3
Effective Communication for Loyalty and Results 83

How to Communicate and Connect
Promoting Honest Communication
Power Listening on the Jobsite
> *Five Minutes—Listening for Results*

Provide Clear Directions
Yelling Is Not (Always) Effective
The Power of "Thank You"
> *Five Minutes—Expressing Deserved Thanks*

The Power of "I'm Sorry"
> *Five Minutes—How to Apologize When You're Wrong*

Ask What, Not Who (Went Wrong)
Encouraging Speaking Up
> *Five Minutes—Showing Personal Interest*

Asking for Help
Push for Information: Drive the Job, Don't Conform
> *Five Minutes—Communicating with the Inspector*
> *Five Minutes—Presenting (Selling) an Idea*

Good Contact Management
Relationships Are Your Payoff

CHAPTER 4

Improving Motivation and Performance 111

Showing Belief and Trust
Five Minutes—Building Confidence in Employees
Removing Obstacles to Motivation
Using Positive Reinforcement
Five Minutes—Motivating with Positive Reinforcement
Recognize Effort, Not Just Outcomes
Five Minutes—Improving Employee Performance
Tips on Positive Motivation of Employees
Pushing People's Limits
Five Minutes—Firing Up Your Crew
Sharing Decision-Making
Five Minutes—Soliciting Quality Ideas
Empowering Employees: Teaching Them to Fish
Five Minutes—Empowering Your Employees

CHAPTER 5

Teaching, Coaching, and Discipline for Accountability 131

Teaching with Patience and Repetition
Five Minutes—Taking Time to Teach
Criticism as a Learning Moment
Five Minutes—Locking in Employee Comprehension
Discipline and Motivation
Five Minutes—Effectively Disciplining an Employee
Warnings that Motivate
Five Minutes—Effectively Counseling an Employee

Deal with Employees in Private
Leveraging Failure
People, Decisions, and Carpet Surfing

CHAPTER 6
Goal Setting for Production and Profit 149
Key Elements for Setting Your Goals
More Goal-Setting Mechanics
Five Minutes—Setting Production Goals that Work
Be Open With Goal Progress
Using Team Goals

CHAPTER 7
Building Teams and Relationships 159
Trust in You = Team Performance
You Lead People and Teams, Not Employees
Five Minutes—Identifying Qualities of Team Performance
Developing Cooperation and Cohesiveness
Ten Qualities of Top Performing Teams
Five Minutes—Promoting Positive Change
Basic Conflict Management
Five Minutes—Resolving Conflicts for Better Teamwork

CHAPTER 8
Mentoring and
Knowledge Transfer 171
    Five Minutes—Sharing Your History and Experiences
    What Does a Mentor Do?
        Five Minutes—Coaching the Apprentice
    Generational Knowledge Transfer
        Five Minutes—Mentoring Your Next-Gen Talent

The Final Word and
Bottom Line 181

Acknowledgements 185

About the Author 187

> **Reader's note:** I use the terms "him," "guy," and "guys" throughout the book knowing full well there are also many outstanding women foremen, leaders, and crew members. For purposes of the book, I use a one-gender approach. For success in the industry, gender doesn't matter—it is all about whoever can earn and keep the job.   *—MB*

Five Minute Lessons

1. Owning Your Title: Professional 47
2. Auditing Your Pro Leader Image 57
3. Five Safety Minutes with the New Guy 60
4. Safety Leadership: Making Consequences Real 62
5. Explaining the Cost of Rework 71
6. Fixing System Failures to Improve Quality or Productivity .. 72
7. Setting Clear Expectations 77
8. Organizing for Effectiveness 81
9. Listening for Results 89
10. Expressing Deserved Thanks 94
11. How to Apologize When You're Wrong 97
12. Showing Personal Interest 100
13. Communicating with the Inspector 104
14. Presenting (Selling) an Idea 106
15. Building Confidence in Employees 113
16. Motivating with Positive Reinforcement 117
17. Improving Employee Performance 119
18. Firing Up Your Crew 123
19. Soliciting Quality Ideas 126
20. Empowering Your Employees 130
21. Taking Time to Teach 133
22. Locking in Employee Comprehension 135
23. Effectively Disciplining an Employee 138
24. Effectively Counseling an Employee 142
25. Setting Production Goals that Work 154
26. Identifying Qualities of Team Performance 163
27. Promoting Positive Change 167
28. Resolving Conflicts for Better Teamwork 170
29. Sharing Your History and Experiences 174
30. Coaching the Apprentice 176
31. Mentoring Your Next-Gen Talent 178

THE FIVE MINUTE FOREMAN
INTRODUCTION

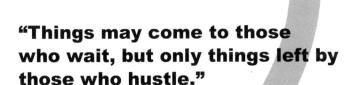

"Things may come to those who wait, but only things left by those who hustle."

—*Abraham Lincoln*

Who **Really** Runs the Construction Industry?

You—the foremen and superintendents of our industry. Rough diamonds.

You do it your own way on every jobsite, in every trade, everywhere in North America. You are tough, loyal, sharp, competitive, ambitious, egotistical, intense, smart, loud, brutal, quiet, confident, humble, insightful, organized, creative, driven, caring, focused, results-oriented, and go-getters. You are coaches, mentors, motivators, and builders—and there are more than 350,000 of you leading an entire industry. Without you, the job simply does not get done.

To get the job done and be a killer foreman in the industry, there are three absolute requirements:

1. You have to work super hard.
2. You have to accept a huge amount of responsibility.
3. You have to make money on your jobs.

There is nothing optional about any of these three requirements. Achieving them will take up every minute of every day. Weeks, months, and years will go by, filled with hard work and the pride of having built great projects.

But what's missing from this grinding career timeline? The opportunity for a foreman to develop himself—to learn, grow, and develop as a professional. To reach his highest potential as a leader. How do you accomplish this? By valuing yourself the same way you value all of the other important things in your life. By taking the time. By making your own development a priority.

Now, a lot of foremen I know are going to tell me they don't need any of that stuff. They understand how to get their crews to work hard. They have been doing the job so long that no one needs to tell them how to run work. And you know what? *I agree.*

So instead of talking about how to run work, how about we find new ways to work on the people side of the business, with benefits that are both positive and obvious?

Just imagine the possibilities…

- Your jobs always make money.
- You never have an accident or injury on any project.
- Everyone on your crews gets along and cares about each other.
- You always complete the job ahead of the schedule.
- You can focus on what you do best all the time.
- You enjoy your job more.
- Every top guy in the industry wants to work for you.
- The people you lead continue to show more initiative, productivity, and loyalty.

All of these might seem too ambitious, or even impossible to some—but you have to imagine what can happen on the job when you are at your very best, at the absolute limit of your talent and powers. You have to think big.

Small actions on your part can result in big change and better results. Even five minutes per day can make a big difference. Few words in this book will be a surprise to top foremen. It's not about information; it's about action. Doing. Something. New. This is the real message and purpose of *The Five Minute Foreman*. My job is to help you reach your potential. Your job is to want to reach it.

So put aside your doubt. Park your ego. Open your eyes and mind. Be confident that you can most likely kick my ass. And take on the challenge of becoming The Five Minute Foreman.

—Mark Breslin

What's in It for **You**: More or Less

I know two things about both of us: One, we like to lead, and two, we can put up with a lot in order to be the one in charge. You have the fire and the passion. My kind of people. The kind of people I want to be a part of helping and developing.

So with that in mind, I wrote this book to help you get more—*and less*—out of your jobs. And both are a payoff.

Let's start with more. I want you to have:

- More productivity and loyalty from your crews
- More interesting and challenging work
- More enjoyment and fun on the job
- More opportunities for advancement and career growth
- More respect from your co-workers, contractors, and owners
- More money and career opportunities.

But there are also some things I want you to have less of:
- Less bullsh** and frustration
- Less stress
- Less time putting up with what you think you cannot change
- Less time worrying about your job
- Less time "firefighting" problems so you will have more time to put towards creating opportunities.

Why are these valuable? Because they make your life better and easier.

Why are better and easier important? I know what it is to be the guy who takes responsibility. I may be a CEO now, but I started in the field doing dirty, lowest-guy-on-the-job grunt work and worked my way up. Like many of you, I worked it out myself. My people suffered plenty while I figured it out. I made every mistake outlined in this book. I was not a real leader until I put in some serious effort to learn. It took me a long time to realize that. My road was not about "better and easier." To now be able to speak to hundreds of thousands of craft workers and actually teach and help tens of thousands of top leaders in our industry is a dream come true—but something very hard-earned.

So as you read on, the bottom line is, I wrote this book because I care about you. And no, you can't have a hug.

Killer Tools for Your Toolbox

This book gives you tools. That's it. Back up the Snap On tool truck and unload that sucker. Hell, you would take as much as they were giving, right?

Well, here they are, as many killer tools as you can use. Just check out the Table of Contents or the list of Five Minute Lessons. Maybe you'll pick two or twenty. But like any tools, they will only help if you use them. So how should you use the tools in *The Five Minute Foreman*? Simple: any way that works for you. It doesn't matter if you read this book all the way through or a little at a time over the next six months. It has to work for you. There is only one key instruction: Read it, do it, practice it. Watch for the result. Repeat.

You'll also notice that some of the book's major themes show up over and over. I don't repeat myself because I'm an idiot. Everyone learns by repetition. So rather than just hope that you "get it," I would rather hit you with a two-by-four on the head over and over again. It was the only way anyone ever got through to me. Hopefully you will be smarter and less stubborn than I was.

Finally, readers may recognize a couple of small bites of material from my earlier books, *Survival of the Fittest* and *Alpha Dog*. I've included them because they contain important lessons that should also be reviewed by any top foreman.

Discipline, Determination, and Room to Grow

As a foreman, you've already achieved a high level of success, and it is a sign of your talent and relentless determination. But showing that you have the ability to grind it out does not help you get to the next level. There is always room to grow.

There's always a new lesson to learn, a new skill to acquire, a new tool to add to your toolbox. The Navy SEALS don't stop training after a couple of successful missions. In fact, when they're not deployed, they spend 90% of their time training and improving their skills. It is about discipline.

An NFL team doesn't skip summer practice after they win the Super Bowl. They keep pushing and improving. The process of constant improvement and self-education is something very common and very powerful in successful people and organizations. Just because construction as an industry has not pushed this as a priority doesn't mean you shouldn't pursue it yourself. It is about determination.

This kind of learning leads to self-pride. That is something that we all want and need; we just don't admit it very often. It is about finding room to grow.

Five Minutes a Day = 21 Hours a Year

Do you do something for yourself every day for your own personal and professional growth? Please tell me you haven't given up on growing your own potential.

A small self-investment every day is the basic strategy of this book. If you spend five minutes a day applying the lessons in these pages, you should become a better foreman, leader, manager, and person.

Five minutes might sound like an unrealistic time frame, not enough to make a difference. Is this just another quick-fix approach like everything else you see sold and packaged for the 3 a.m. TV crowd? No. This isn't a pitch for some lame infomercial.

I found out a long time ago that you hard-core construction foremen are not easy to convince. The concepts have to prove themselves to you. So the test is this: If you spend five minutes a day working on yourself, you will see changes not only in yourself but in the people who work for you—and damn quick, too.

So why five minutes? Why not ten or twenty? Because at five minutes…

- Anyone can do it.
- No one can say, "I don't have the time."
- It doesn't interfere with what you are already doing.
- Over an entire year, investing just five minutes a day equals more than twenty hours of self-development.
- Doing anything better motivates you, boosts your morale, and shows your best side to the people who work with you.

If you can hang with that five minute commitment, I promise you will develop new habits. You'll see that changes in approach create changes in the performance of others. Not every lesson will apply to you. Each foreman has a different set of existing skills and talents. That's fine. Choose the ones that really strike a chord and commit to turning those lessons into actions on the jobsite. Say the words, execute the actions. Make it happen.

Five Minute **Obstacles**

Doing something different just once for five minutes is easy. Doing something different for five minutes every day is hard. How do you keep adding a little more to your abilities and ambitions every day? By believing that you are worth it. By believing that you are a very talented person who can and will continue to grow your abilities. This book is really an exercise in valuing yourself at a higher level in life.

You also have to recognize that once you commit to a course of self-improvement, obstacles will show up. A lot of times it will feel as if you're getting in your own way. These obstacles might include:

- Sticking with old habits
- Staying with "This is the way we've always done it"
- Fear of change
- Discomfort or embarrassment
- Worrying about what others will think
- Thinking you are giving up power
- Stress or time pressure
- Success (the belief that already being good at something means you don't have to try to improve).

Some of these obstacles are not about your performance but about you worrying how others might judge you. When you try to do something different, people might look at you funny or question you. What can I tell you? That's just part of the deal. It has to be about you first.

Self-improvement is supposed to be uncomfortable at first. That's why so many people don't do it or seem negative when others try. But guess what? It's not about them. And if they are not sincerely supporting your growth and goals, they are not worth listening to anyway.

CHAPTER 1

THE TEN FACES OF THE FEARLESS FOREMAN

"Don't tell me how rocky the sea is, just bring the ship in."

–Lou Holtz

A top foreman must play many roles. The challenge is knowing when and how to adapt. There are many ways to lead, but for a foreman who wants to excel, the following ten key identities will serve as a very good foundation.

1. The Bad Ass with Purpose

Even a bad-ass foreman has to have a reason for being a bad ass. Professionals always have a purpose over and above just getting the job done. This purpose is the underlying theme of everything they do. It is something that provides the "big picture" for their efforts and fuels their enthusiasm.

I would like to share with you my thoughts on the purpose of a professional construction foreman.

The purpose of a professional construction leader and foreman is:

> To build *people* into remarkable performers
> To build these performers into amazing *teams*
> Who then build high-quality, *profitable projects*.

Note that people and teamwork come before the work or the money.

If you want to think "big picture" on your job and in your life, remember that your purpose rises above all else. The job always gets done one way or another. Money is made or money is lost. But along the way you will end up making a big, big difference to the people who trust you to teach, coach, and lead them.

2. The **Protector** of Life and Death

Perhaps the most important part of being a construction leader is ensuring a safe jobsite. Your leadership can make the difference between life and death.

A leader takes responsibility for the safety and well-being of those who work for him, regardless of what he thinks about them. There are only a few occupations left where people put their lives in harm's way, and construction is one of them.

This standard is one of personal and professional responsibility. If you compromise safety, someone will pay the price—in pain, injury, or even death. I have been on jobsites where multiple fatalities have occurred. I have seen the bodies. I have seen the sorrow and second-guessing. I have seen foremen and contractors crushed under the weight of regret. I have seen guys hang it up because they didn't want the responsibility anymore. But guess what? It was too late to turn back the clock.

Many years ago I was trained by guys who didn't take safety seriously. Maybe when you were coming up it was considered unproductive or not macho to follow safety rules to the letter. I didn't pay attention to the safety policies or the rules the contractor asked me to follow. No. I learned by watching my foreman. That is what determined my behavior. That is what determined my actions. That was the root of many unsafe acts I stupidly engaged in. That was "old-school" thinking that today has nearly been eliminated.

I know that today's safety procedures can sometimes seem like overkill, and the messages can get repetitive after a while. But it's up to you, as a leader, to explain to your crew why there is absolutely no compromise when it comes to safety. There can be no exceptions either—for anyone. It is not about just making them follow the rules. We're back to the people skills side of the business again: You have to get them to share your mindset that safety is a great thing, that it is good for everyone, and that they should believe in it fully. That is the way to create the right environment for safety excellence.

Get them to understand and then believe.

The bottom line is this: You are in charge of life and death. Your crew has to know that you are serious about safety—not because you enjoy giving them a hard time, but because you care about them and their families. You want them to go home safe and healthy. Let them see that you take their safety personally. It's about the brotherhood of the job. It's important for them to understand and believe—but it has to translate into them taking care of each other. You are the only one on that jobsite who can really get them to invest in and care for each other.

The difference between life and death is in your hands.

3. The **Big Money, Big Responsibility** Leader

Most foremen have no idea how important they are. They often still think of themselves as blue collar craftspeople. That is so wrong in so many ways that I don't know where to start. But the real place to measure foreman responsibility is in dollars.

The story of the dollars should convince you that foremen like you are high-level, serious leaders and managers. Please let me prove it to you. If you complete just one exercise in this book, make sure it's this one.

The Five Minute Foreman

Answer this question:

What is the total dollar volume that a top foreman or superintendent will manage in a thirty-year career? Please do this math.

Annual Volume Managed: $ _____
                          × 30 years
                       ─────────────────
                     = $ _____

$300 million
$250 million
$200 million
$150 million
$100 million
$50 million

$10 million per year × 30 = $ 300 million
$5 million per year × 30 = $ 150 million
$3 million per year × 30 = $ 90 million
$1 million per year × 30 = $ 30 million

1 yr   5 yrs   10 yrs   15 yrs   20 yrs   25 yrs   30 yrs

Think about those numbers and *get serious*. Your actual amount will vary depending on your industry and the size of contractor you work for. But the dollars managed by a foreman over the course of thirty years can easily total $30 million…$50 million…$200 million…even *$300 million or more.*

That's *one foreman* managing tens or even hundreds of millions of dollars worth of:

- People
- Money
- Schedules
- Materials
- Risks
- Safety
- Client satisfaction.

That's more responsibility than 90% of white-collar business people will ever have in their lives. A top foreman will often make more independent decisions than most business college graduates working in some cubicle for a big corporation. A foreman lives on the high wire. He is a serious professional who calls the shots almost all the time. In summary:

Big money.
Big responsibility.

Get your mind wrapped around owning your new title: ***Professional Construction Leader (PCL).***

4. The "Sink or Swim" Graduate

Now that we've established that a top foreman has huge responsibilities, let's travel back into your history. How did you get picked as foreman? Chances are it was for one or more of these reasons:

- Hardest worker on the crew
- Smartest craft guy on the team
- Most ambitious
- Natural leadership ability
- Tommy didn't show up
- Hated working for others.

No matter how you became a foreman, you probably went through the "sink or swim" school of training. That's when a contractor takes the best guy he can find and then chucks him way out into the middle of the swimming pool of the jobsite. If the guy swims to the side and brings the job in, he gets to be the foreman. And if he drowns? "Well, tough sh**, kid—we'll find someone else and chuck his ass in."

If you are a foreman today, I know that you swam to the side. You made it. So, here might be the most significant question of this entire book:

HOW MUCH LEADERSHIP AND MANAGEMENT TRAINING DID YOU GET AFTER YOU SWAM TO THE SIDE OF THE POOL?

    a) Zero
    b) Nothing
    c) Nada
    d) Oops
    e) WTF?

More than 95% of foremen report that they received ZERO professional leadership or management training.

So let me see if I understand this: As a contractor, first I'm going to take a great guy out of the field and off his tools. Then I'm going to give him zero leadership and management training. Then I'm going to turn over anywhere from $20 million to $200 million worth of work to him and make him figure it all out for himself. Is this correct? Is this your story?

WHO WOULD BE CRAZY ENOUGH TO RUN A BUSINESS LIKE THAT?

Only the entire construction industry.

Foremen have had to figure it out for themselves. Foremen have had to forge themselves into successful leaders. This do-it-yourself model is a hard way to go, and it's bad business, too. It takes too much time, effort, stress, and trial-and-error. "Sink or swim" is a lame excuse for the development of talent like yours. You deserve better. Now is the opportunity to grow.

5. The Moneymaking Machine

The ability to create a successful financial outcome for each and every project you work on is *a primary job requirement* if you want to build a career as a foreman.

If you can't make money, you can't stay.

The key is to understand that there are many different ways the foreman makes money. The ability to meet a schedule and stay within a budget estimate are two obvious skills every foreman needs to succeed, but there are others that are just as crucial.

Long-term success with profit generation is also achieved by mastering the "people skills" side of the business. You have to get your crew to *want* to make money on the project. You have to get them thinking as you do: Every dollar matters, every minute counts.

There is widespread thinking on a lot of jobsites that the contractor is a bad guy because he is making money. What kind of bullsh** is that? His risk. His money. His equipment. His ass. He might do well. He might go broke. He put you in charge as foreman for the purpose of making money off all those resources. So getting your people to understand and support the idea that making money is the name of the game is an important part of mastering the people side of the business. They have to buy in as players and not just spectators. They have to accept the idea that making money is good for everyone—and not resent the contractor or you for pushing hard to make it happen.

6. The **Cocky SOB**

A professional is expected to be confident in both words and actions. A crew wants a confident foreman. But there is a fine line between someone who believes in himself and someone who is over-confident.
The industry needs someone who not only shows confidence but also breeds that in others. Super-capable, but not arrogant. Not abusive. Not above everyone else. Someone who has the power, knows it, and uses it very wisely.

But he probably also has a damn high opinion of himself.

7. The Compassionate **Giver**

Being a professional requires you to be a giving person. This never makes you a soft or weak leader. The strongest people in this world are often those who are capable of giving the most.

Being a giver at work is kind of like being a human ATM. When's the last time you went to get cash from an ATM and it spit out blank pieces of paper instead? Never. Unless it's broken, you can count on an ATM to give you what you ask for: money, something of great value. And it gives it to you on a reliable, consistent basis.

In many ways, a professional foreman is like that ATM. Unless he's sick or injured, the contractor and the crew rely on him to give them something of value day in and day out. Every time they ask for it. On demand. What are they looking for?

- Direction
- Encouragement
- Guidance
- Coaching
- Expertise
- Problem solving
- Structure
- Decisions
- Mediation
- Advice.

A professional foreman who gives is someone who operates from a strong set of values. Integrity, honesty, an unwillingness to pass the buck, caring, compassion, fairness—these make up the "values blueprint" that a foreman uses to build his career and his relationships. A good leader is someone who realizes it is only through his giving that others can reach their potential. Giving is probably the ultimate foundation of the professional foreman—the ability, desire, and capability to give until it hurts.

8. The Enforcer

At the end of the day, there is only one person on the crew responsible for making sure that company policies are followed and everyone behaves professionally. That person is the foreman…also known as The Enforcer.

The Enforcer is not a friend, a pal, or a coach. You cannot use your buddy status with The Enforcer. The Enforcer is the guy the crew knows will not compromise on key policies or company values. They know that if they push, there will be push-back. They also know that if they go over the line, they are going home.

The Enforcer does not exercise power just because he can. He uses it to keep people in line and to prevent them from doing stupid things. He is both feared and respected. A guy unable or unwilling to be The Enforcer is going to deal with a lot of complications while trying to be only the good guy.

9. The Winning Coach

No team ever won anything with a bad coach.

Lots of above-average teams have won everything because they had a winning coach.

Here is what that winning coach looks like:

- Disciplined
- Demanding
- Detailed
- Enthusiastic
- Instinctive
- Decisive.

Motivating, managing, and placing talent in the right place to succeed—that's a winning coach's approach. He breeds loyalty. He breeds commitment. He gets the best out of people. He coaches for results. And it's a great approach for you as a top foreman.

10. The Role Model

The most influential and visible way everyone on the jobsite learns is by watching you. Whether you like it or not, you are a role model, just like the guy on the front of the Wheaties box or the sports hero your kids look up to. That comes with some responsibility. It really is something you have to live up to.

Role model. Totally cool. The guys will never say, "Hey, I want to be like you, man." Not out loud, anyway. But you sure want them to think it.

CHAPTER 2

PROFESSIONALISM, SAFETY, INTEGRITY, AND QUALITY

"You moon the wrong person at the company party and suddenly you're not a professional anymore."

—Jeff Foxworthy

Now that we have reviewed the many sides of being a top foreman, the remainder of the book will teach you how to master the people side of the business. There are quite a few lessons on the road ahead. Just to give a sample of what it takes to master the people side, let's look at some core areas of competence that really are mandatory for a professional foreman. These all serve the people side of the business in a big way:

- Motivation
    - Coaching
        - Communicating
            - Listening
                - Conflict resolution
                    - Training
                        - Teambuilding
                            - Mentoring
                                - And quite a bit more.

ON PROFESSIONALISM

Consider your new title, **Professional Construction Leader (PCL)**. Can you own that?

It may sound like a weird question, but it should be answered honestly. Just because someone has an important title, rank, or rate of pay doesn't automatically make him or her a professional. The title PCL is something you have to earn, and it's also a state of mind.

So really, what or who is a professional?

A PROFESSIONAL IS SOMEONE WHO LIVES UP TO THE FULL POTENTIAL OF HIS OR HER CAPABILITY AND JOB TITLE, NO MATTER THEIR LEVEL OF EDUCATION OR THE INDUSTRY IN WHICH THEY WORK.

In most professions, a person also reaches the top of the career path through a lot of studying and development. Professionals like doctors, accountants, lawyers, nurses, police officers, dentists, and others expect to spend a lot of time *learning* before they get a chance to actually *practice*. This ongoing learning requirement is something that *should* also be a part of being a PCL. Even if it is only five minutes at a time.

Blue Collar **Businessperson**

The average small business owner does around $800,000 in annual volume. That defines his or her financial responsibility. Maybe, just maybe, you manage more than that. Maybe a lot more. What's the point? You are managing more money and responsibility than millions of small business owners across North America.

You are not just a construction guy.

You are not just a blue collar guy.

You are not a trade or craft guy.

You are a businessperson.

You need to understand that you really are in the position of business management. You may identify most with whatever trade you are coming out of. If someone asked you what you do, would you say ironworker, carpenter, electrician, sheet metal worker, pipefitter, boilermaker, operator, painter, insulator, or other trade? Probably. But that's no longer good enough. That was then, and this is now. The correct answer is, "I'm a businessperson."

FIVE MINUTE LESSON

Owning Your Title: Professional

It's fitting that the first Five Minute Lesson is about your own identity and learning to see yourself differently. It is totally okay to raise your self-image. It's not about trying to be more than you are; it's about accepting who you are now and who you can be in the future. The ability to believe this, inside yourself, is the stepping stone to the rest of your self-development.

Do This/Say This:

Today, before you get out of your car or truck, look at yourself in your rearview mirror and say these words: "I am a professional." Then say it one more time: "I am a professional." You think this is lame, right? This sounds like some kind of weird activity? You're thinking, "I'm not going to do this." I get it—but if you don't say it and believe it, why should anyone else?

Those words are going to sound strange, but no one will hear them except you.

Remember, this first exercise is the foundation for everything to come.

To be it, you have to **think it**.
To own it, you have to **say it**. **"I am a professional."**

You have to say it until it doesn't sound strange to you anymore.

The Contractor-Foreman
Partnership

If your contractor gave you this book, it probably means he feels the same way I do. He cares—about you, about his company, and about the future of the industry. I know—you're rolling your eyes and thinking, "Yeah, if the contractor loves me so much, he can just pay me more money." But look at it from his perspective. If you were in his shoes, would you rather have a motivated, self-directed, growing leader or a guy stuck at status quo?

The simple fact that you have this book in your hands means that someone values you. They realize that you need more time, money, and effort spent on providing you with leadership and management tools. So—better late than never. Yes, this business is about making money and being successful. But you and your contractor should have the exact same goal. Your success and his success are tied together. It is a partnership for and about success.

The **Professional**: Mastering the **People** Side

We started this section with you owning being a professional construction leader. What did we learn? That it begins with you. The choices you make. The ways you see yourself and others. So two roads go on from here. Here is a final summary of things to remember as you set your nav system for professional leadership and mastery of the people side of construction:

A Professional...	A Faker...
...is honest about his shortcomings and works to improve them.	...tries to hide his shortcomings (and usually fails).
...understands that people create productivity and that determines a project's success.	...believes success is determined by factors outside of his control.
...knows that it's not about making people work hard but about making them WANT to work harder for you personally.	...believes that you have to constantly berate people to get the most out of them.
...motivates using praise, recognition, goals, and teamwork.	...motivates by yelling and reminding everyone who's boss. Praise is for the weak.

A Professional...	**A Faker...**
...understands that construction is a people business with some tools and materials thrown in for good measure.	...thinks about the work more than the people.
...never begins a sentence with, "Back in the old days we did it this way..."	...acts like he is back in the old days.
...knows that effort is contagious. When one part of the team gets recognition for their effort, the others will want to pick up the pace.	...worries that telling people they did a good job will cause them to slack off.
...identifies people's limits so that he can push them past those limits.	...identifies people's limits so he knows how little to expect from them.
...isn't afraid to involve others in the decision-making process, but knows that in the end, the buck stops with him.	...never lets anyone in on the decision-making process because the less they know, the better.
...isn't afraid to do his share of "sh** work" after he's promoted to foreman.	...thinks that becoming foreman means he never has to do "sh** work" again.

Ten Affirmations for the
Pro Foreman

An affirmation is a fancy way of describing talking to yourself. But affirmations are also about telling yourself the truth in a positive way. You want to have the right things running through your mind—and that is what a positive affirmation is all about.

1. I don't stop learning once I become a foreman. There is always room for me to improve.
2. I am not afraid to admit when I'm wrong. I'll get ten times more respect when I own up to a mistake rather than try to hide it.
3. I can never be afraid to ask questions.
4. Even when I don't think someone is watching, I will act like someone is.
5. My work ethic determines everyone else's effort.
6. I am worthy of the title of foreman. I accept the responsibility of leadership.
7. I am relentless. I am like a shark: always moving forward. Especially when there's an unexpected delay or obstacle.
8. I am open to any and all input to help me improve.
9. I am not above anything or anyone.
10. My real power comes from doing the right things for the right reasons, not from my title or the ability to tell others what to do.

The **Pro Presentation:**
What the Customer Sees and Hears

You've heard the phrase, "You can't judge a book by its cover." That may be true, but you can often judge a *foreman* by his cover—that is, his overall appearance, including how he chooses to dress on the job. Now, I can already hear the grumbling: "Breslin, this is total bull***t. We are in construction. Who cares what we wear as long as we get the job done?"

Go ahead, get it out of your system. I'll wait.

Finished? Good. I really don't care what you think. I care about *what the customer thinks*. The person or company that hired your contractor—yeah, their opinion matters. Because you are a living, breathing, straight-up representation of the branding and professionalism of your contractor.

A top-level foreman distinguishes himself from others with a good presentation. You can't look like a homeless guy on the job. You can't look like a construction hobo. When you're dressed appropriately, you identify yourself as a leader, not just to your crew, but to the contractor and customer as well. You may not like it. You may not think it's fair. But it's reality.

There is another part to pro presentation: how you sound. Hey, I cuss plenty—both in this book and in life. It is not absolutely necessary, and there is definitely a difference between a few choice words and ten f-bombs a minute. All I'm saying is pay attention to how you sound. Don't ever "dumb yourself down" to fit in. Don't ever think that you have to cuss excessively to be a hard ass. Remember that people judge your intelligence and your professionalism based on the words you choose.

Presenting Yourself
as a Leader

What follows are four hard-earned bits of wisdom. Picture yourself sitting down to a big dinner with a table filled with veteran foremen. What would they tell you about presenting yourself as a leader? What advice would they give? I guarantee these four ideas are going to come up at least once. All of them deal with presenting yourself as a leader.

1. **Someone is always watching your performance.** It's really hard to keep yourself accountable when you're the one in charge. In fact, that's why some foremen totally blow it: They forget (and stop caring) that anyone is watching. Your performance as a leader is visible to everyone. This thought process keeps you grounded and humble.

2. **Someone is always listening.** Words have a lasting influence. If you're like me, you can remember mean or negative things people said to you years ago. Words are so easy to waste. They are so easy to let fly. *But they define you.* A foreman's words weigh heavy. Here are a few key points to remember:

   - Never criticize the contractor or badmouth the owner in front of your guys.
   - Don't bitch about the work, the inspector, or anything else. Don't be a hater.
   - Don't talk about other people or their personal lives.
   - Don't gossip or badmouth people.
   - Don't bully or tease people. If it's hurtful, stupid, or mean, it's not funny. Don't be an asshole just trying to get a laugh.

3. **Be a boss first and a friend second.** If you are friends with people at work, then your employees will consider you a friend first and a boss second. That's just how it is. And everything that happens on the job is now personal. If your employees see you as their friend first, they are going to expect different or special treatment and take any critical feedback very personally.

   This is just a case of confusion. Because you play two roles, your employees are going to pick the one they like best. When you bounce from friend to boss and back again, they have a harder time than you do, especially because they don't like to be treated as an employee first.

   I have a very serious commitment to my employees. I would do anything within reason and my resources for them. I am totally committed to their success. But I am not their friend first and never will be. And they know it. And they act like it. And no one gets confused. And sh** gets done with no drama on that front.

   Friendship and business often don't mix well. Make sure that you set the bar early and often with employees. No special breaks. No double standards.

4. **Don't party to excess with your employees.** You give something away when your people see you wasted. You have to see it from their perspective.

   You are the person in charge. You are the authority figure. You are the example to live up to at work… and then you go out with them and become someone totally different. You may do or say things that don't put you in the best light.

   When it's time to go back to the job, it's just another day—for you. But what you might underestimate is how your employees see you. Most foremen would say that it doesn't matter. But if they saw their own boss drunk off his ass, would they still have the respect and even fear that should come with that position?

FIVE MINUTE LESSON

Auditing Your **Pro Leader** Image

This exercise is about seeing yourself through other people's eyes. You are the pro on the job and often the only representative for the company. You might be the main liaison with the general contractor, inspector, owner rep, or OSHA compliance officer. So, while your own self-image is definitely important, how others see you also matters a great deal, especially if you hope to move up the career ladder.

Do This:

Before you leave for work, do a quick check. *Think about what the client would see* **and how a professional would appear. Ask yourself the following questions:**

- Am I doing a good job of representing the contractor's reputation and brand with my appearance?
- Would someone be able to tell that I'm in charge of the jobsite just by looking at me?
- Would I listen to or trust a guy dressed exactly like me?

Understanding the Construction
Business Model

For graduates of the "sink or swim" school of foreman development, there are usually a few gaps in knowledge or training that are hard to overcome without direct instruction. If you want to really understand the business model you are in, then there are things you need your superintendent or contractor to share with you. This is by no means a complete list, but it is presented so that you can see how much there is to learn and understand:

- How does the bidding process work from beginning to end?
- How do you put together a schedule?
- What are the most common ways we end up in trouble on a job?
- How do we calculate overhead and what is in it?
- How does safety relate directly to insurance costs and profits?
- How do you figure out the profit margin on a job?
- How do you determine what it will cost, in real dollars, if the project comes in late by a day, a week, a month, etc.?
- How do you finance the purchasing of equipment, tools, vehicles, etc.?

These are things you can ask your contractor to explain if you want to really understand the bigger picture. Or you can attend a foreman training program that focuses on the business challenges that are contained in many of those questions. Great stuff.

ON SAFETY

Most foremen have extensive experience with safety management. Safety is number one at most companies, and we have already hit the key theme of life and death. If that doesn't motivate you, I am not sure what will. So what follows are two lessons to act on in the field for results.

The first is for the newest player on your team who has to get "with it" ASAP. The second is for the most experienced guys who may think they already have heard enough on the subject of safety for a lifetime.

Both can be very powerful tools. Use them well.

FIVE MINUTE LESSON

Five Safety Minutes with the New Guy

Based on all available materials and statistics, the person most likely to be involved in an accident on your jobsite is a new employee. Therefore, a small amount of extra time spent with that person is likely to be a great investment in jobsite safety.

Most of the time, the new person has, at the very least, gone through a basic safety orientation. Your five-minute exercise involves supplementing that basic info with a quick personal reminder.

- Before the new person goes out on the job for the first time, you are going to pull him aside or meet him as he shows up.
- If you are busy with something, ask him to wait. Don't let him start work until you have the following discussion.

Do This/Say This:
"I want to make sure you understand our safety rules. Did you review the safety orientation materials?"
[Probably "Yes"]

"Do you have any questions?"
[Probably "No"]

Professionalism, Safety, Integrity and Quality

"So I want you to understand that the key hazards out here might include _____. [Fill in the blanks here with the items you, as a foreman, believe are the most dangerous. This will change from job to job. It's important to give the new person specific hazards relative to the project at hand. Don't just recite the same two or three general warnings over and over again.]

"Also, you need to know that we are damn serious about safety, and I won't overlook anything unsafe that anyone does, including you. Finally, there are no stupid questions—if you have any questions or concerns about safety, then come to me. Got it?"

These five minutes protect the person, the crew, and the company. And the new employee is the guy (or girl) who needs it most.

FIVE MINUTE LESSON

Safety Leadership: Making Consequences Real

There is a big difference between talking about safety and getting the guys to understand what happens when the team fails. This exercise is about getting your crew to understand fully the real human consequences of jobsite accidents. Today is about convincing the crew to watch out for each other.

Do This:

- Use your weekly Safety Tailgate Meeting for this exercise.
- Ask who on the crew has been on a job where there was a serious accident, injury, or fatality.
- Have them tell the story.
- Ask them if they heard what happened to the guy afterwards or with his family.
- If you have a similar story, add yours as the final wrap-up.
- Don't be surprised if almost every guy on the crew has a story like this.

Say This:
"We are not letting this happen to us. We are out here to watch out for each other. Everyone has to have everyone else's back every minute. We don't let things slide. We don't make excuses for each other. You know what can happen to anyone and the impact that can have on them and their family. That is not going to happen to any of you on my crew."

ON INTEGRITY

Integrity, Honesty, and
Visible Values

It's hard to find many leaders who value honesty and integrity anymore. You can't even turn around these days without seeing some senior-level businessman, politician, or church leader who is supposed to be a great leader acting like a jerk-off lying sack of sh**. And do you know how most people react? "Ho-hum. So what? What else is new?" That's not good…and it's definitely not good enough for a professional construction leader.

There can be quite a bit of dishonesty in our business. No one likes to talk about it, but you know what I mean:

- Padding hours on time cards
- Leaving early
- Lying to cover your ass or someone else's and escape the blame
- Damaging something and not owning up
- Stealing materials
- Drinking on the job
- Getting hurt on off-time and filing a claim as if it happened at work.

Professionalism, Safety, Integrity and Quality

It is part of the world we live in. But it doesn't mean we have to just "go along to get along." As a foreman, one of the biggest challenges you will face is figuring out where to draw the line between what's cool and what is absolutely, positively unacceptable. If the crew sees you compromise your honesty or integrity even one time, they get the signal that it's okay for them to do the same thing. Every action you take on the job—whether it's interacting with your crew on the jobsite or talking to the client or contractor in an office trailer—reflects upon your integrity.

Some leaders have "situational integrity." They will at times bend the rules, leave out certain pieces of information. They will tell themselves it's not a big thing—it's just this one time. It's just this situation. And that is the biggest lie of all: the one you tell yourself. When you skim over the truth, you leave a little bit of your honor behind.

There is another big excuse we tell ourselves: "The other guy is doing it too." He is? Really? Okay, well then, let's all be dirt bags and diminish our own personal integrity and honor.

When mastering the people side of the business, all I can say is, integrity pays. It builds trust. It instills confidence. And it breeds more of itself.

Accepting **Responsibility** (and Blame)

A great leader protects his people and does not throw them under the bus. This can also mean that sometimes you take heat even when it's not your fault.

My preference is for my team to trust me and believe that I have their backs. In the past, I have covered for my team and taken the blame—when it was their fault. Nothing else I have done has ever generated more loyalty.

Here's my thinking: If I don't cover them, they are simply going to worry too much about making a mistake and getting their asses chewed. Is it upsetting when I have to take a bullet for someone else? Yes. Am I pissed? Yes. Will I take that bullet repeatedly? No. If someone is unable to generate total commitment after I throw myself under the bus for them, they don't belong on my team. It's as simple as that. But accepting leadership responsibility means taking it on for your entire team. It's a part of mastering the people part of the business. When you have your team's loyalty, you have everything you need.

Treat People **Fairly**

One of the hardest lessons I ever had to learn about leadership is the importance of treating everyone fairly—which also means treating everyone the same. When I started to lead, many things influenced how I treated people:

- Did I like them more than others?
- Did I dislike them personally?
- Did they have challenges and issues in their life?
- Did they make more money or generate more opportunities for the company than others?
- Was I personal friends with them?

At one time or another, I let all of these questions influence me. The end result? I ended up managing everyone differently. I thought I was being more effective because I was giving people individual attention. But I was wrong. By not treating everyone the same, I looked unfair—one of the worst mistakes a leader can make.

Here's what it looked like to my employees:
- Favoritism
- Disinterest
- Lack of support
- Double standards
- Cutting slack for personal issues (for some people, but not all)
- Inconsistency in decision-making
- Exceptions to every rule.

It can be very difficult to treat everyone the same. It can be super hard for you to treat your friends at work the same as the people you don't really even like.

But stick with it. Ride out the bumps in the road. If your goal is a high-performance team that takes your lead and doesn't look at each other with envy or disdain, make sure you treat everyone fairly and equally. Being consistent and fair creates trust.

ON QUALITY

Schedule, Quality, and Rework

One of the biggest challenges for foremen is balancing schedule vs. quality. In other words, they struggle with getting a job done quickly while still maintaining a very high degree of quality.

In tight markets with small margins, time can often win out in the battle of priorities. Foremen give in to the clock. They "just want to get finished" and meet the deadline. If that means cutting a few corners, well, no biggie.

The price paid for compromising on quality isn't always obvious, but it can be extremely costly to a company. What kinds of costs are incurred by compromising quality standards?

- **Call-backs for rework.** Rework is the most expensive unanticipated cost associated with almost any construction project. Rework costs have more impact on profit than nearly anything else. And guess what? Your crew determines the amount of rework through the quality of their work. Always stress to your crew the vital importance of getting the job done right the first time. The goal is always zero rework.

- **Client dissatisfaction.** A client paying top dollar who gets marginal quality is not going to be happy. In the construction world today, more and more work is negotiated instead of bid. That means the relationship and reputation of the company have a real value. Poor quality erodes client confidence. This leads to a poor reputation, a weakened brand, bad word-of-mouth around the industry, and loss of leverage in the contractor-client relationship.

- **Liability impacts, such as latent defect claims.** This is when the owners eventually come back and sue the contractor years later for poor quality. They didn't notice it at the time, and everyone has moved on...except the lawyers. This drives up insurance costs significantly.

The tension between quality work and schedule is very real. Foremen tell me all the time that they feel under more pressure to meet schedules than to install perfect work. The decision on high production and high quality is almost always in the hands of the foreman. It is a discussion worth having with the crew—but do it before the job (or the call-backs) begin.

FIVE MINUTE LESSON

Explaining the Cost of Rework

The cost of rework is a major hit to the contractor's bottom line. It is the result of employees not really understanding the impact that a poor-quality job can have on the project and the company's reputation.

This exercise is about education and behavioral change. There is a lot of pressure to "go fast" in the business, but such an attitude often results in quality control issues that require call-backs or special attention. The crew needs to be made aware of this.

Do This/Say This:

- Tell the crew that zero rework is the goal on every job.
- Explain how the cost of the entire job gets hammered by rework.
- Tell them that the cost of rework is at least three times the cost of installation.

FIVE MINUTE LESSON

Fixing System Failures to Improve Quality or Productivity

Many times, what appear to be people problems are actually system failures. The employee is doing what he or she can to make it work, but the system that's supposed to be supporting them is failing. It's easy to simply blame the employee for the problem and ignore the system failure. But top foremen need to constantly be on the lookout for ways to *improve* systems, not just accept them as-is. You should also make it clear to employees that they, too, are expected to point out problems with the system, not just shrug them off. Even better, ask them to suggest solutions. Ignoring system problems inevitably leads to higher project costs.

You will be surprised how much great feedback you can receive when your crew starts thinking seriously about how to improve systems.

Do This/Say This:

- Identify a problem on your job, with your crew, or in the company.
- Ask your crew, "What is standing in the way of us doing a better job?"
- Listen for ways the systems can be improved.
- Set up a quick meeting with your boss (or send him an e-mail).
- Present the ideas for improvement to your boss and outline the benefits.
- Tell your crew what you are doing to try to improve the system.

Focus on the Customer

Construction is a relationship business. Yeah, from the outside it looks like it's all about building stuff—but relationships are what make all of that activity profitable. There is no relationship more important than the one with the customer.

A lot of guys don't really even think about the customer. For them, it's all about working for the contractor and getting the job done (and depositing that paycheck every week). But someone is ultimately paying the bills. Everyone is actually getting paid by the customer. And you are often the main person on the jobsite at whom the client is looking when determining if they made the right choice in hiring your contractor.

How you act with and respond to the customer has lasting effects. Quality, safety, and integrity are not just buzzwords—they are what the customer is expecting and paying for. Remind your crew of the importance of creating a great impression on the owner of the project in every way. This is the branding of your contractor, your crew, and yourself. Make it a worthy and noticeable brand.

Concentrating on What's
Important

A professional foreman must learn how to develop and apply laser-like focus. In a nutshell, to develop intense focus you have to recognize that trying to do a bunch of things at once reduces your effectiveness. This is hard when you have fifty things on your list. This is also the big problem with multi-tasking. Many people buy into the lie that multi-tasking is a great way to work all the time. In reality, to get stuff done, often the exact opposite approach is the way to go. You have to stay focused on what is most important and knock it out.

Besides just having too many things to do, what else gets in the way of concentration and focus? Life. Pressure. Stress. Things beyond our control. We all have days where we don't feel like bringing our best, but a foreman must constantly focus at work. Forget the fight you had with your girlfriend the night before, or being up half the night with a sick child, or not sleeping or feeling well.

Guess what? Time to suck it up.

A pro accepts this. Apprentices and journeymen might get to indulge in their "issues" of life from time to time. But there are different rules for the professional foreman. He knows that if he lets his focus drift he'll lose momentum, get distracted, and begin to make decisions that are not reflective of his best efforts.

The legendary basketball player Julius Erving, or "Dr. J" as he was known, put it this way: "Being a professional is doing all the things you love to do on the days when you don't feel like doing them." That is a great summary of what it takes to maintain focus and concentration.

This all seems like common sense, but focus directly impacts your ability to master the people side of the business. If you aren't able to monitor your own thoughts, feelings, and behaviors, who can? Focus is the "one thing at a time" approach. Focus is about finding ways to shrink down your point of concentration.

FIVE MINUTE LESSON

Setting Clear **Expectations**

Setting expectations gives employees an exact description of what you need and want from them. This helps them focus on what is important. Too often leaders expect their people to be mind readers. They are not. If you want them to do a good job, they have to know exactly what you want.

Areas where clear expectations are important might include safety, housekeeping, quality, break times, pre-planning, tardiness, material storage, client interaction—almost anything that is performance related.

Do This:

- Identify a segment of work, a certain behavior you want to see, or an outcome you desire
- Go to an employee or group of employees.
- Be very specific about what you expect from them.
- Ask if there are any questions.

Say This:

"Here is exactly what I expect and what it looks like to me. If there is any reason you cannot or don't think you are going to accomplish it, I want to know about it immediately, not when it is too late to do anything about it."

Open Minds Drive **Innovation**

The following sentence should not be used at work, when having sex, or generally any other place in life:

"But that's the way we've always done it."

Positive change does not come about by leaning only on traditions and legacy. Change comes from being open-minded. Positive change comes from pushing aside the belief that whatever we have always done is good enough.

Be an open-minded foreman. Give your people the breathing room to come to you and each other with innovations. Innovation can improve:

- Quality
- Schedule completion
- Communications
- Customer satisfaction.

Not every suggestion for innovation is going to make a big difference. Some ideas might even be stupid. A few will be brilliant. If you are the guy worrying that someone else's idea might make you look bad, you're missing the real opportunity. What do you think happens to you when all the great ideas that the company adopts come from your crew?

Be open-minded and clear-eyed. Keep asking, "Why are we *still* doing things that way?"

Connecting Paperwork and **Profit**

I know—most everybody hates paperwork. If you ignore it or pretend it's not important, however, you're just setting yourself up for failure.

Paperwork is as important to contractors and clients as tools are to the craftsmen on the jobsite. Businesses run on paperwork. Without the proper documentation—receipts, work orders, change orders, and the like—nothing moves. Not equipment, not supplies, not workers.

But most importantly, without the correct paperwork, the contractor won't get paid and runs the risk of not getting properly reimbursed for all of the costs he has incurred on the job.

Learn to love it. Or hate it less. Just know that it matters. A lot.

Five Tips for **Documentation**

Documentation is a necessary and strategic part of jobsite supervision. It is absolutely critical in situations where job directives, owner payment, schedule adjustments, or other agreements have been made at the site of construction. You find that many very important conflicts, including lawsuits, end up depending on the foreman's jobsite documentation, job log, or diary. To support good documentation, here are a few good basic habits to practice:

1. Always carry pen and notepad (or iPad).
2. Get in the habit of writing things down immediately. You can't remember it all. If you don't jot it down now, you will probably forget it.
3. Use your smart phone to record things that you don't have time to write down right away and then transcribe them later.
4. Keep a complete daily diary of each project you work on, regardless of whether the contractor or owner requires that you do so.
5. Get the inspector, engineer, owner's rep, or anyone else authorizing work, scope, schedule, etc. to sign off on all changes, cost issues, and related matters. It is not okay to just take people's word for it when it comes to significant changes that cost a lot of money.

FIVE MINUTE LESSON

Organizing for Effectiveness

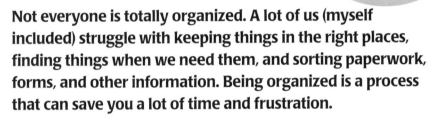

Not everyone is totally organized. A lot of us (myself included) struggle with keeping things in the right places, finding things when we need them, and sorting paperwork, forms, and other information. Being organized is a process that can save you a lot of time and frustration.

You may be asking, "How does this impact the people side of the business?" In two key ways. One, you are an example to your crew. If you are organized, it will rub off on them. Two, organization is incredibly important on any jobsite. It has a direct impact on productivity, the schedule, and often safety as well. If things aren't running smoothly, chances are there is a lack of organization somewhere along the chain of command. When was the last time you ever heard an owner or contractor say, "Yeah, the foreman is totally unorganized, but it doesn't matter, because everything is running so smoothly"?

Do This:
- Decide when the best time is for your five minutes of organization.
- Dedicate yourself to organizing one thing really well.
- Spend a full five minutes or more on your target area.

If you spend five minutes a day for one week focusing on becoming better organized, you will see a payoff. Take it from a former unorganized guy who had a lot of excuses.

CHAPTER 3

EFFECTIVE COMMUNICATION FOR LOYALTY AND RESULTS

"Communication—the human connection—is the key to personal and career success."
—*Paul J. Meyer*

If you want to be an outstanding foreman, becoming a great communicator is essential. In fact, pretty much every major lesson in this book has something to do with communication—either with others or with yourself. As a foreman, if you can't communicate in a real, honest way with your contractor or your crew, then…how can I put this politely? Oh, right: You're screwed.

For some reason, though, a lot of guys walk onto the jobsite and simply forget how to communicate effectively. They refuse to adapt to the person or situation. They are stuck on "what works for me." They just communicate in whatever way works for them and let the chips fall where they may. Their attitude is, "Tough sh** if you don't like it. Grow a set already."

I know that construction workers aren't always the most communicative people in the world, but guess what? **Communication dictates performance**. Powerful and effective communication is all about using the right words in the right way at the right time. Every situation is different. Again, it's not just what you say to your crew, it's *how* and *when* you say it.

How to **Communicate and Connect**

Good communication is really about *connecting* with the other person. In *Everyone Communicates, Few Connect*, leadership expert John Maxwell defines connecting as "the ability to identify with people and relate to them in a way that increases your influence with them."

Now here's where things get a little awkward for foremen in general and guys in particular. In order to connect with the other person, you are going to have to become more comfortable with being open. You can't have a real connection without emotion. This runs right into the wall of the construction tough guy code we have all learned at one time or another.

To get people to do what you want on a consistent basis, you have to show them you are personally invested. Guys will walk through fire for a foreman who cares about them and engages with them at a personal level.

This is difficult for many of us, to say the least. It's a lot easier to yell or make a sarcastic remark than to let guys know that you are sincere or that you care. The odds are that the vast majority will respond positively if you communicate—if you *connect*—in the right way. In summary, be present, be real, and be open. No one can take away your authority or power, so don't be insecure about it. It's not a guy thing, but that doesn't mean it doesn't work. Practice it. It gets easier.

Promoting **Honest** Communication

We already covered honesty in action in a few places in the book, but when applied to communication it is absolutely critical. Why? Because one failure is always going to be remembered and trust is always going to be in question. The foreman is on point with employees, other contractors, inspectors, and vendors. When communicating, do not bend, fold, or mutilate the truth.

Sometimes we fool ourselves into thinking we need to lie. Or maybe we just drift into that "gray area" a little. Reasons vary, but mostly we lie to:

- Avoid discomfort
- Avoid accountability
- Make ourselves out to be more than we are
- Take advantage of an opportunity
- Avoid being judged.

Most of these are pretty lame excuses and don't really provide a huge payoff. All I can offer is this: When you know someone has lied, does it change how you feel about him? Probably. Do you trust him less? Probably. Do you respect him less? Probably. Does it get in the way of effective communication? Yes.

Does it prevent leaders from mastering the people side of the business? Absolutely.

Power Listening on the Jobsite

Listening, according to my employees, is one of my worst skill sets. I am impatient. I want to know *now*. Just give me the bottom line. Don't tell me some boring-ass story. I finish sentences. Talk over people. Interrupt. I think I know where the discussion is going to end and jump there. What an idiot. I know it's wrong and I *still* do it!

This tendency has caused a lot of lost time, ill will, pissed-off employees, and more mistakes than I can count. For a long time I just didn't value listening. Now I do. Why? Because *listening creates power*.

Two-way communication is the key to smooth operations on the jobsite. It is also the only way you will know you are doing a good job.

In order to be an effective listener:

1. Don't text, type, read, or multi-task while trying to listen. You are telling the other person he is not important.
2. Don't display impatience: It makes people nervous and they leave out key information.
3. Don't roll your eyes or sigh like the person talking is the stupidest person on the planet.
4. Don't start thinking about what you are going to say when the other person is done talking—concentrate and really listen to him.
5. Don't interrupt, no matter how boring the other person may be.
6. Don't try to finish someone else's thoughts or sentences.

And here are simple things you can do to become a power listener:

1. Stop whatever you are doing when an employee approaches you to talk.
2. Give the person your undivided attention.
3. Turn your body towards him.
4. Look the person in the eyes.
5. Don't react until you have heard the entire (or most of the) story.
6. Try not to let your head explode but exercise patience.
7. Repeat back what you heard to reconfirm.

FIVE MINUTE LESSON

Listening for Results

Listening is often hard for people in charge. If you're used to telling people what to do all day long, every day, you end up doing most of the talking. You have to make a real serious effort to stop and open your ears to what is going on around you.

Today's exercise is five minutes of power listening. What is power listening? A great-sounding phrase I made up to get your attention. But now that I have it, let's try the following:

Do This:
- For five minutes you are not going to tell anyone what to do. You will not interrupt, look at your phone or radio, or do anything else but listen.
- Ask an employee, vendor, or subcontractor an open-ended question that relates to the job.

Say This:
- "How do you think we could do better on _____ _____ [any key subject]?"
- "If there is one thing that we could do that would improve production on the job, what do you think that would be?"

It may seem strange to actually think about listening, but sometimes you have to schedule time, put aside distractions, and resist your tendency to roll over people so you can hear what they are saying.

Provide **Clear** Directions

Good communication is clear communication. This is also a skill that took me a lot of time and effort to learn. My theory used to be, if you don't know what I want you to do by ESP, then you are too stupid to work for me. When I would get busy, I would give people terrible direction. What did that look like?

1. Partial instructions
2. No specific deadlines
3. Never asking if they had questions after I told them what to do
4. Never asking if they understood what I had said
5. Giving them the task without explaining the ultimate goal or reason for doing it.

Providing clear direction to your crew is relatively simple, but it requires discipline. Though there is a Five Minute Lesson for improving in this area, it is so important I include this additional blueprint for the next time you have to tell someone what to do:

1. Give the person your undivided attention.
2. Give instructions with the appropriate level of detail.
3. Ask him to repeat a summary of the instructions back to you.
4. Ask him if he has any questions.
5. Give him the timeline or deadline for the task to be completed, and ask him if he will have any problems meeting it.

Yelling Is Not (Always) Effective

Next to the sound of tools, equipment, or machinery grinding away, yelling is probably the most common sound you will hear on a construction site. And guess what? Sometimes yelling is great. It blows out the old deposits and charges up the adrenaline. Yelling can be very appropriate in cases of danger or stupidity. Ass-chewing is fine, and in certain circumstances you have to do it. I have, and it works.

But yelling at people as a normal method of direction is bad business. It wears you out, and it wears them out. Worst of all, yelling at people generally is more about YOU than THEM.

"Serial yellers," as I call them, use yelling as a power trip, a way to show everyone who's boss. Many yellers and screamers are insecure. Yellers try to gain power through intimidation. Fear is their leverage. Teams can be driven this way, but the problem is that they are 100% *externally* motivated. Take away the yelling and fear, and what do you have?

- People afraid to make a mistake
- People less inclined to take initiative
- People waiting to be told exactly what to do so they don't get yelled at
- People who perform differently when the whip is not being applied
- People who are resentful and angry underneath.

If the people who work for you are so stupid that they absolutely cannot get anything done without you yelling at them, get new people. Other than that, remember that yelling is not an effective communication style.

One last note: For over a decade I studied martial arts under a teacher (sensei) who was also an Olympic coach at the Colorado Springs training facility. He was the most dangerous man I ever knew. He was also one of the most soft-spoken. When he told me something, softly and directly, man oh man, you can bet your ass I was listening. He never yelled. He didn't have to.

The Power of "Thank You"

"Thank you" is a great tool in a foreman's communication toolbox. "Thank you" equals respect. "Thank you" is another way of saying, "I care about you." It says, "I am paying attention. I don't take you for granted." It's also common courtesy. We teach our children how important it is to say, "Thank you." But then sometimes we act like children and think we don't have to say it at all.

When you thank someone, you are connecting with him in one of the most personal and positive ways possible.

Saying "Thank you" has become a regular part of my personal success. If I had to guess, I would say I have sent more than 1,000 thank-you notes in my professional life, and I've made another thousand personal thank-you phone calls. And you know what? I probably should have made a lot more, because nothing I've done in the industry was my accomplishment alone.

Every week there are employees, friends, clients, and others who do stuff for me and deserve recognition. I found out a long time ago that a sincere thank-you never gets forgotten. Most people take others for granted, so the person who makes the small extra effort gets a huge benefit for being thoughtful.

This is not just about being polite. This is about showing the most basic level of care for people.

FIVE MINUTE LESSON

Expressing Deserved Thanks

The expression of any form of thanks is rare on the construction jobsite. Some guys think it's weak. That's ridiculous. Didn't your momma teach you any manners?

Today we are going to work on the very simple concept of saying, "Thank you."

- Look around the jobsite for people doing great work.
- Look for vendors kicking ass for you.
- Look for anyone helping others do their work well.
- Look for people making a notable effort (trying) to do a good job.

Do This/Say This:

"Hey, man, I really want to thank you for _____."

- Use the person's name. This makes it personal and real.
- Look the person in the eye. This is how he knows you're being sincere.
- Describe exactly what it is that you are thanking him for.
- If you're thanking him for something he did that was really significant, consider shaking his hand. This signifies that he really has made an impact and that you are raising him up to your level of respect.

If you do this, you will have just hit a home run. Don't even think about it. Don't even argue with me. It is huge. Please just say, "Thank you." Today. Every day. Get in the habit. It works.

The Power of "I'm Sorry"

Let's get this straight right from the start. There are a lot of times in life when we should say that we are sorry but we don't. The challenge is not really about *when* to say it—it's just two words, after all. We almost always know when we should say it. For a foreman, the hard part is *knowing it's okay to say it in the first place.*

You should immediately say "I'm sorry" if you have been:

- Stupid
    - Offensive
        - Wrong
            - Rude
                - Inconsiderate
                    - Defensive
                        - Short-tempered for no reason.

The biggest problem most people have with saying they're sorry is that they are embarrassed and pissed off that they put themselves in such a situation to begin with. They know they should apologize, but they begin a thinking process that sounds like this:

- It wasn't so bad.
- It was partly their fault.
- I didn't really mean it.
- The other person should be able to "take it."
- If I ignore it, no one will remember anyway.

Most people do not want to go through the discomfort and embarrassment of an apology. But I'll tell you a secret: If you are wrong, everyone already knows it.

Two years ago, before a big presentation in the Midwest, I was stressed out and distracted. I was also rude and abrupt to a guy and didn't even know it. Over a year later someone mentioned to me that the guy was really angry about how I treated him. So, fourteen months and 2,000 miles later, I got his number. I called the guy up and apologized on the phone. I said, "Hey, man, I am really sorry. That is not who I really am, and I need to pay closer attention to how I treat people sometimes." For a moment there was dead silence. Then he said the words that made it all worthwhile: "Mark, that goes a long way with me." He was a good man to cut me some slack.

Suck it up. Say you're sorry. Mean it. Be sincere. Don't put in any excuses or whiny bullsh**. Saying you're sorry lets everyone move on.

FIVE MINUTE LESSON

How to Apologize When You're Wrong

Is this obvious and easy? If it were, more people would do it more often.

How to say you're sorry and apologize goes like this:

Do This/Say This:
- Understand that the only thing you are trying to do is say you are sorry.
- Do not go into it expecting everything to be perfect or to get the other person to tell you that everything is fine. You are doing this because it is the right thing to do.
- You have several ways to open this. Here are a couple:
  a) "Hey, I think I screwed up the other day. I wanted to apologize for _____."
  b) "You know, after I had time to think about it, I could have handled that situation with the _____ _ a lot better. I'm sorry about that. Really."
  c) "After that problem / issue / question we dealt with the other day, I did a little more homework. I guess I jumped the gun a little. I'm really sorry that I _____ _____ without thinking it all the way through."
  d) "Dude, um, pretty sure that I was a total asshole the other day. Sorry."

Ask **What**, Not Who (Went Wrong)

When a mistake occurs, how about asking, "What is the problem?" before you ask, "Who caused the problem?"

Oftentimes, especially when I am pissed off, I start looking around for the person or persons responsible for the mistake, problem, or delay. Someone has to die. Someone has to pay. On occasion I have gone off on someone who I thought was the problem only to find out later it was the system that failed him.

Do not automatically look for someone to blame as the cause of the problem. Sometimes it's people, sometimes it's the system, and sometimes it's you.

Blaming without analysis kills morale and confidence among your team. You can also end up looking like the asshole who doesn't really know what's going on.

Encouraging **Speaking Up**

Speaking up ("up" as in "up the chain of command") in our industry isn't always easy. Members of your crew can be reluctant to bring something up to you. And you might feel uncomfortable having to talk about some tough issues with your contractor.

But sometimes there's no way around it. A lot of times it is the very best thing to do. That's why your crew has to know that it's okay to speak up. This is also an absolute necessity when it comes to safety.

Create a "safe zone" for people to ask any question or make any suggestion.

Make it clear there are no stupid questions and there will be no negative repercussions for raising your hand and asking for any clarification.

Making it easer for folks to speak up can have huge benefits. Unsafe conditions on the jobsite can be identified and eliminated. An employee who is using drugs, drinking to excess, or otherwise being a danger to himself or others can be dealt with. If crew members know they aren't going to get yelled at or publicly embarrassed for saying something, a lot of times they will point out quality issues that can be fixed before a call-back is required.

They have to feel they can come to you.

FIVE MINUTE LESSON

Showing Personal Interest

These simple exercises will help you show your employees that you care about them and are personally invested in their happiness and well-being. This leads to loyalty—and loyalty leads to increased levels of commitment and productivity.

Do This/Say This:

- Tomorrow, greet members of your crew by name first thing in the morning.
- On Friday afternoon, before everyone leaves, ask crew members about their weekend plans (or kids or family).
- On Monday morning, follow up with at least one crew member about his weekend and see how things went.

You don't have to do this every time if you think it will seem forced or insincere, but if you can do it with any consistency, it will communicate a personal interest that translates to greater loyalty coming back to you. Simple. Basic. Important.

Asking for **Help**

Since the construction industry is made up of mostly guys, the phrase "I need help" really doesn't work. Why? **Because guys don't ask for help**. We don't even ask for directions! We need to be seen as strong and in control at all times. We don't want to be seen as unable to do anything for ourselves. A lot of guys learn early on in life that asking for help is the same as admitting that you are weak. This is not true. It's counterproductive and based in feelings of insecurity.

I am an Alpha personality. I don't have any problem making up my mind. I can be a little intense to work for. But despite all that, I still ask for help all the time. I ask for help in solving business problems, sorting out issues with various people, looking for new ideas, you name it. Starting a sentence with, "Hey, I need your help on something…" is at least a weekly if not daily occurrence for me. My team doesn't think I'm weak because I ask for help; they think I respect their ideas and input.

What is the benefit for me personally? I don't want to carry the load for the entire team every minute of every day, every year, forever. Especially because some of my team are strong enough to depend upon. There have been a few times where challenges in my own personal life required me to ask for some help. Better to ask than to crash and burn. It's not about bringing your "issues" to work all the time. It's about knowing when you need to lean on others. So for me, it's still hard to ask for help—but I also know that when you ask for someone's help it builds a bridge between the two of you. Also, it is very difficult for anyone to turn down someone who asks for help.

Finally, it is worth thinking about the consequences of *not* asking for help. Most people I know who have trouble in their personal or work life should have asked for help a long time ago—and in most every case, they have friends, family, or co-workers who would have rallied for them without question.

Push for **Information:**
Drive the Job, Don't Conform

Information has incredible value for a project. The amount of important information you have often makes all the difference between you driving the job or it driving you. Ask for—or (politely) demand, if necessary—that you have the following on your projects:

- Complete set of drawings
- Revised drawings
- Addendums
- Clear description and understanding of project's scope
- Complete specifications
- Key contracts and subcontracts
- Contact information for owner reps, engineers, inspectors, etc.

Make it clear from the outset—preferably during pre-job planning sessions—that you really need a certain amount of information before the project begins. Don't just conform to whatever comes down the pipeline to you.

Finally, you've heard the phrase "Garbage in, garbage out," right? It means that the quality of the information you receive will often determine the quality of the project. If you don't have the proper amount of information going in, the end result can be compromised.

FIVE MINUTE LESSON

Communicating with the Inspector

The best foremen in the industry are those who understand how to build relationships that work. Relationships need trust, communication, openness, and flexibility. While not every inspector or owner rep will respond to these qualities, it's still important to demonstrate them on a consistent basis.

If you go into a situation with a defensive or negative attitude, you'll wind up causing the other guy to respond in the exact same way. If you expect problems, you'll get problems. Try to be the positive standout among everyone else—the one guy people know they can trust.

This exercise will help you develop your ability to connect and communicate with the project inspector or owner's representative. Your relationships with these folks are extremely important and can have a huge impact on the outcome of a project, so you need to work at them. You need to have a plan.

Do This:

- Today, approach the rep/inspector during lunch or a break.
- Remember that others in your position have likely burned him before, so he may not be 100% interested in trusting you.

- **Understand that the rep/inspector may initially want to exert some kind of power or authority. Don't let that get in the way. You are not in a contest.**
- **Try to approach him with some degree of personal connection. Be observant to what he might be interested in outside of the work at hand.**
- **Build a connection based on your intent to do a great job and make him look good, too.**
- **Do the little things that don't cost a lot and don't compromise your position. If you want to have a decent transactional relationship, you have to show some form of willingness on your part.**

No matter how good the interaction and dialogue are, make sure you document, document, document.

FIVE MINUTE LESSON

Presenting (Selling) an Idea

Often when you're working on a project, your knowledge and experience will enable you to see how certain things can be done better, easier, or cheaper than the original plans specify. These improvements can wind up saving the contractor or owner a lot of money—but only if you are able to present your ideas and suggestions in a professional manner.

Here are some ideas on how to persuade an inspector to go along with a change or adopt a new idea.

Do This:
- Think through how you want to approach the subject. How exactly would your idea work? What are the first questions someone in the inspector's position would ask? Have you thought through all of the consequences of this idea?
- Think about where you want to bring up your idea: out in the field? in the contractor's trailer? in the break room?
- Make sure you pick a time when the inspector is not distracted or under pressure.
- Talk to the inspector and lay out your idea in a clear and easy-to-understand way.

Say This:

"I have an idea I want to run by you. I think if we do this _____ [idea or change] we can save time, money, or whatever else...."

- Make sure to emphasize the most important benefits of your idea (saving time, saving money, better quality, trade-offs, etc.).
- Give him time to make the decision. Tell him you will follow up, and let him know you are available at any time to discuss the idea further or answer any questions.

Good **Contact** Management

This one is short and sweet. Make sure that you are very sharp on your contact management skills. You can't communicate with someone if you can't find him. As you meet people on the job, get into the habit of immediately requesting their contact information. Proactively insert the names, phone numbers, and e-mail addresses of key people and organizations into your smart phone, notebook, job diary, iPad, or whatever else you are using. Have the following contact information at your fingertips:

- General or subcontractor representatives
- Inspector or resident engineer
- Owner's representative
- Key vendor office numbers
- Vendor's delivery guy's cell phone numbers
- Relevant unions and business representatives
- Closest local hospitals and industrial medical clinics.

Relationships Are Your Payoff

Good communication skills will make you a better leader and enhance your productivity. But the ultimate payoff is that you will see a major improvement in the quality of your relationships, both personally and professionally. You cannot have a stable, high-level relationship with someone without good communication. If you can't figure out how to talk to one another, there is no relationship, period.

Take marriage. Show me a successful marriage and I will show you two people who keep working on how to communicate with one another in a respectful, positive way. Show me a failed marriage and I will show you two people (or at least one) who lacked the ability or desire to communicate effectively and honestly (that lesson cost me about 50% of my assets).

On the job, the same is true. The better the communication, the higher the level of trust and respect. Yes, it takes some effort. Yes, it is always easier to just do it on your own rather than reach across the great divide and ask for help. But the payoff is worth it: developing strong and lasting relationships that result in more money and more success for everyone, not just the guy at the top of the ladder.

CHAPTER 4

IMPROVING MOTIVATION AND PERFORMANCE

"Leadership is the art of getting someone to do something you want done because he wants to do it."

–Dwight D. Eisenhower

Motivation is an extremely important part of your job as a foreman. When it comes to mastering the people side of the business, this could be the biggest moneymaking skill of all. Let's start out by defining what motivation is and what it isn't.

- Motivation is all about the **people**, not about the work.
- Motivation is about **affecting behavior**, not about working faster.
- Motivation of others is based on **the use of every tool** that you have available to you.
- What motivates you **will not necessarily be what motivates others**.

Showing Belief and Trust

Here are six very powerful motivational words a leader can say to someone:

"I know you can do this."

Most people have some type of insecurity, and they naturally bring it to work with them. When challenged by situations, the question of whether they have the ability to excel may stand as a barrier to their performance.

If someone you respect tells you he believes in you and trusts you with a certain amount of responsibility, I guarantee that you are going to make a serious extra effort to get the job done right. Belief and self-confidence can drive production.

FIVE MINUTE LESSON

Building Confidence in Employees

Today's Five Minute Lesson is dedicated to building confidence in your employees. Whether it is your best or worst employee, confidence-building is a critical leadership skill.

Do This/Say This:

Today, do the following:

- Choose one person on the crew who you feel has the ability to produce better results.

- Take this person aside, away from the rest of the crew. Say this: "I need to tell you that I think you can be even better at what you are doing. I see a lot of guys in this business, and I'm telling you that I believe in your ability."

You want him to borrow your confidence and make it his. It is okay to tell another person you believe in him. It does not make you sound weak. It pushes him from the inside. If you really want to see how it works best, try it with your spouse or kids.

Removing Obstacles to Motivation

In a national survey by William M. Mercer Inc., a quarter of workers surveyed said they could do 50% more work. On average, almost all workers reported that they could do at least a little more work. That's a lot of lost productivity and money. Clearly these employees have another gear that is not being engaged. What are the obstacles preventing them from being more productive?

It turns out that you have to remove the barriers to motivation before you can start taking actions to boost production and the quality of work.

Here are the top three reasons for underachievement given by employees in that survey:

1. **Lack of recognition or rewards for a good performance.** This responsibility falls directly on you as a foreman. It doesn't have to be dollars; it has to be a reward of some sort. A word, a gesture, recognition, a material action—it always matters. Doing nothing is the obstacle. If you don't give people a reason to improve their performance, they often won't.

2. **Lack of ownership or involvement in decision-making.** Asking people for input creates buy-in. Buy-in creates loyalty and commitment. A top leader gives his team ownership; he gives them a voice. Again, doing nothing in this area kills initiative and ownership and motivation.

3. **Lack of opportunity for advancement.** Try to point out the connection between job performance and advancement as often as you can. Use your crew's ambition and desire for upward mobility, more hours, more security, and a better life as a way to motivate them.

Using Positive Reinforcement

How long does it take to hear about it when you mess something up in this industry? Ten seconds? But how long might you wait to get the praise or recognition you deserve for a job well done? Years, perhaps. More likely, forever.

Praise and recognition are very powerful motivators in the workplace. Almost every professional study will cite them as the number one way to get better performance out of people. Despite this, our industry is a place where praise and recognition are rarely given out.

Part of the problem is that past generations—the "old school"—didn't value praise. Toughness and self-reliance were the ways to earn respect. Praise was for the weak. Praise would raise expectations or make people want more money. Praise might actually make the guy feel good about himself or his performance!

So we kicked praise to the curb.

So guys in construction do not value or use much positive reinforcement. The impact of this is pretty obvious. If you don't use the most powerful motivator in the entire workplace, then what do you get?

Lower production. Lower morale. Lower level of loyalty. Lower profits.

Now, I know there are many foremen who will say that they can drive people to be their best without using praise. Maybe they're right; maybe they've figured out the magic formula. You can ramrod people and need to from time to time. I have done it myself with great results. But that doesn't mean you have to ignore the power of the positive.

All I can tell you is every study and every available fact show that praise and recognition have both short- and long-term benefits. Use praise and recognition daily. It improves performance and makes money.

FIVE MINUTE LESSON

Motivating with Positive Reinforcement

Today you are going to use the number one motivator in the workplace: positive praise and recognition. This happens to be a great tool to boost confidence, productivity, buy-in, morale, and loyalty. And even better, it does not cost you or the company a dime.

Using praise is rare on the job. A lot of focus is often on the negatives. So this requires you to be very deliberate and try something different.

Do This/Say This:

- Catch someone doing the right thing. Look for a crew member who is performing very well, producing a great outcome, or making a major effort.
- Go up to that worker and look him in the eye.
- Tell him what he has done to make a positive impression on you. Be specific. Don't give him a general "Atta-boy, way to go" pat on the back. Say this: "[Name], you did a great job on _____ [specific description of quality, speed, teamwork, or other]. I really appreciate it."
- Watch his face and eyes for the reaction. I guarantee you'll like what you see.

"Old-school" thinking in our industry says, "Why should we have to kiss someone's ass so they will do their job?" Effective leaders say, "Why wouldn't I use every tool possible to motivate my guys?"

Recognize **Effort,** Not Just Outcomes

Giving an employee or your team credit doesn't always have to be about the outcome. When you see someone *really trying hard,* he too may be deserving of recognition. A good example is the apprentice who may not have the skills yet but is busting his ass nonetheless. This is an excellent time to encourage him. Many times in the workplace it is the encouragement that comes when you are *not* succeeding that is the most motivating.

FIVE MINUTE LESSON

Improving Employee Performance

The worst guy on the job has the greatest potential for improvement.

The only questions are, Does he have the capacity and desire to improve? And is he worth it?

Many times, the answer to both questions is yes, but no one wants to put in the time and energy it takes to turn the guy around. Today we are going to try to solve this problem and get a lot more out of this person.

Do This:

- Identify a low performer or underachiever who you think has significant potential to improve.
- Go to the person and pull him aside at the beginning or end of the shift.
- Instead of treating him like an idiot (or someone you are going to fire tomorrow) try to think of him as a potential asset.

Say This:
"Look, I know this is going to be hard for you to hear, but you are not getting it done on this job. I'm not saying this to be an asshole. I am trying to help you. Here is what I am seeing: _____." Then list the problems you have observed with the person's performance or attitude. Be specific, and hit the major things—don't overload the person with a dozen criticisms.

When you are finished, ask: "Do you understand what I am saying? So let me finish this with one question for you. What do you think you can start doing differently or better tomorrow that will be visible to me and the rest of the crew?"

If he turns it around even a little, keep working on him. If the guy really doesn't get it, or doesn't want to get it…then get rid of his ass and find someone worthy to put your energy into.

Tips on **Positive Motivation** of Employees

1. **Be sincere.** Construction guys have the most powerful B.S. detectors in the world. They know when someone's trying to get over on them.

2. **Don't go overboard.** When a guy does something worthy of praise—is proactive, shows initiative or fast thinking, offers up a suggestion to increase productivity and efficiency, etc.—don't act like he just discovered a cure for cancer. Be enthusiastic. Be honest. You're not trying to manipulate him with false praise and flattery—you're trying to motivate him based on the fact that he is showing the right behaviors.

3. **Be specific.** A good formula for a motivating phrase is PRAISE + SPECIFIC DETAIL. It's not enough to just say, "Great job." Adding the performance detail helps them know exactly what they did right.

Pushing People's **Limits**

Another important way to motivate people is to push them beyond their self-imposed limits to show them they can do a lot more than they thought they could—to help them set a new bar of performance for themselves. Most people don't even know what their real limits are because they won't push themselves that hard. Or they are afraid to fail.

A good foreman needs to determine each employee's limit. Every worker is capable of different things, so trying to make everyone reach the same level isn't always the best approach. On a typical crew, you'll most likely have a mix of the following types of people: superstars, rookies, underachievers, and so on. Each one has a different ability to produce, and it is worth identifying what his general operating limit is first—then you can start to push each one beyond his individual limits.

My goal as a leader is to make sure that everyone who works for me does things they didn't think they were capable of. The ability for them to push beyond their limits is a combination of the following:

- The foreman has to give the person the opportunity.
- The foreman has to know the person is probably going to fail before he succeeds when pushed beyond perceived limits.
- The foreman must understand that self-confidence is often the main barrier to going beyond perceived limits.

FIVE MINUTE LESSON

Firing Up Your Crew

Top coaches in every sport have a special speech they keep in their back pocket. They only pull it out when they really need it. It might be the ninth inning in a playoff baseball game, the final seconds of a championship hockey game, or in the corner before the final round of a boxing or UFC match. This special speech churns the emotions. It's filled with words that fire people up and help them focus—words that generate results.

But this speech only works on special occasions. If you give it all the time, you just sound like a rah-rah guy. You have to wait for the right day, when the time has come for some serious action—when it's time to fire up the troops.

Do This:

- **Get yourself in a mindset to be really into it.**
- **Think about the words you want to use, but not too much—you want your emotions to be what they really hear.**
- **Call the crew together and tell them to pay close attention.**
- **Maintain eye contact with the entire group as you speak—move from person to person.**

Say This:
" I don't make speeches very often. I don't like to. But there comes a time where you guys have to hear what I am thinking. And what you need to hear is this: _____
_____ "

Options might include:

- "Today we are going to get the highest daily production this company has ever seen."
- "Today I want to see guys running. I want to see you guys pushing harder than you ever have."
- "We are behind on this schedule and it's time to fix that problem. I know we can catch up, and today is the day we are going to start doing it."
- "At the end of today's shift I am going to call the office and tell them what our production was today, and I want to blow every other crew in this company away. I know we can do it."

Be forceful and honest. This is a push message. This is a "You can do more and better" message. This is a "You need to look inside yourselves" message. It is not about pleasing *you*. It is about pushing *them* to perform at their highest level. Right NOW. You want to light their fire, not bawl them out. Show some emotion. Show some passion. They might be slightly freaked out when you are done. Good.

Sharing Decision-Making

If you want people to perform at a higher level, then help them own the outcome. If you are making decisions and involve others, they will have a personal stake in the success or failure. On the other hand, someone who is being told what to do has no personal stake in the outcome and will tend to just go through the motions for their paycheck.

What kind of stakes are we talking about? Pride in ownership. Shared accomplishment. Team achievement.

Ninety percent of the foremen I've worked with don't involve others in decision-making. They see it as giving away power. But you're not giving away power; you're sharing it. And by sharing power, the foreman creates team momentum.

Again, the barrier here can be ego or authority or discomfort. People will not lose respect for you when you involve them in decisions. Their respect will increase, and so will their buy-in and effort to support you and the team.

FIVE MINUTE LESSON

Soliciting Quality Ideas

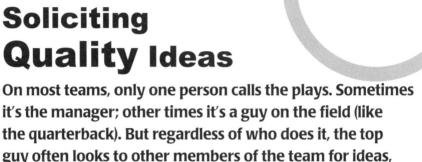

On most teams, only one person calls the plays. Sometimes it's the manager; other times it's a guy on the field (like the quarterback). But regardless of who does it, the top guy often looks to other members of the team for ideas, information, and inspiration. He's smart enough to know that he doesn't always have all the answers.

Every single day of the last twenty-five years I've spent leading others, you can be sure that I have asked for ideas. It's the main way I lead. I have no problem telling people what I need, want, or expect. As a top-performing foreman, you need to be able to do the same. But more often than anything, I ask for their ideas and input. That's the subject of this exercise.

Do This:

- Pick a job-related topic that you think your crew will be interested in. Maybe it will be a discussion about the schedule, a certain safety aspect, or a particularly difficult task that is coming up. The point is, choose something you think will stimulate discussion. You want the first time to be a success.

- Explain the topic clearly and then ask for their input.

Say This:
- "What do you (guys) think about _____?"
- "How can we get faster, better, higher quality, safer, etc…?"

Then listen. Let them explain their ideas. Ask questions. Take out a pen and take a note or two. Encourage the "quiet types" to come out of their shells and help them along. Don't shoot them down. Don't criticize, comment, or analyze. Afterwards, thank everyone for their input.

Again, you are not giving up power or authority. You are looking for buy-in and quality input.

Empowering Employees: Teaching Them to Fish

How many times a week does someone come up to you for help on something that you know he should handle himself? Most foremen tell me it happens several times a day at least. That adds up to roughly 500 times a year when a foreman has to stop what he's doing and deal with problems or issues that other people bring to him. If I've just described your daily routine, then you have to break that cycle.

Why do they keep coming back? Because they think you can fix anything? They think you're amazing? No, they keep coming back *because you've trained them to come to you and be dependent on you.*

The old saying, "Give a man a fish and he eats for a day; teach a man to fish and he eats for a lifetime," is the best management advice you can get. **Teach your employees to fish.**

It will help you recapture **100 hours a year** of time you would normally lose on the job doing things for others that they should handle for themselves.

In the pressure of the moment, the easy thing to do when these employees come to you is to give them the answer. Fix the problem. Put out the fire. All of those actions are just giving the person a fish. At the same time, you are training them not to think for themselves and to be overly dependent on you. The best response is to try to get them to first think and act for themselves.

FIVE MINUTE LESSON

Empowering Your Employees

"Empowering" means giving your employees the ability to act in a proactive way without getting their heads chopped off by you, the boss. This lesson is really about a combination of delegation and encouragement. It is also about training them to stop coming to you for every little thing—and training you to resist solving everyone else's problems.

Do This/Say This:
- The next time someone comes to you with a problem, pause. First ask what he has already tried.
- Second, ask him what he thinks the options are.
- If he doesn't have answers to #1 and #2, send him away until he does.
- Repeat.

This simple process will retrain your employees to be more responsible and independent. Again, it will give them a chance to "learn to fish" so that they don't have to come to you all the time. At first, it can be very hard to watch them flounder around and seem to waste time. What is likely is that they will become more self-sufficient and develop better judgment overall—key to saving you time and headaches.

CHAPTER 5

TEACHING, COACHING, AND DISCIPLINE FOR ACCOUNTABILITY

"A good objective of leadership is to help those doing poorly to do well and help those who are doing well to do even better."

—*Jim Rohn*

Teaching with **Patience** and **Repetition**

"Didn't I tell you this ten times before, you dumb sh**?"

Another construction learning moment. Not polite. Not very effective. But it contains a lesson. For people to learn, they must have repeated exposures. Like learning your ABC's or tying a shoe, learning new skills or applied knowledge usually takes a few tries, corrections, and improvements.

Telling someone to do something repeatedly usually leads to the belief that the person is as dumb as a rock. That is likely incorrect. Repetition is an important learning tool.

BUT…

If you do it with spit flying and your face purple with frustration while you repeat the instruction, that probably isn't helping all that much.

The enemy of learning is impatience.

FIVE MINUTE LESSON

Taking Time to Teach

Today we are going to focus on properly teaching someone to do something. This requires a combination of time, patience, and process.

Teaching may take up the entire five minutes or even a lot more. With some irritating people, it may seem like a lifetime. But teaching someone to do something properly has a lasting business benefit.

Do This/Say This:
- Identify the person whom you would like to instruct.
- Tell him you want to take a minute to show him / train him on something.
- "Show and tell" when you are teaching—make sure he sees everything you do and that you explain each step in the process.
- Ask questions about his level of understanding while you are showing and telling. You want to make sure he gets it.
- **_Remember that people generally only remember 10% of what they are told verbally_**—most people are visual learners who learn by seeing and then doing (this is especially true in construction).
- Conclude by asking him to repeat back what he was told.

Criticism as a Learning Moment

When you criticize people, make sure it is a stepping-stone to improved performance. Don't criticize just to make people feel bad. Ask them what they did wrong. Ask them what they should have done. Most importantly, ask them what they are going to do differently next time.

I've never understood foremen who only yell and scream at people and expect that to fix the problem. How is that supposed to help them improve? The people I admired most and wanted to work for the hardest were those who could tell me with nothing more than a silent look that I wasn't measuring up. Disapproval can be a powerful motivator if the person respects his supervisor. *But he still needs to know what to do differently next time.*

FIVE MINUTE LESSON

Locking in Employee Comprehension

How do we know that people understand what we are telling them? Maybe they nod. Maybe they look at us a certain way. Or maybe they don't know what's going on and don't want to admit it.

Today we are going to work on confirmation and affirmation. Sounds simple, but it can really save a lot of time and money.

Do This:
- Give an employee instruction on what you want him to do.
- Ask him to repeat back what you just told him

Say This:
"O.K. Did you get that? [He says yes.] O.K., repeat back to me what you heard me say."

This is the best way to avoid mistakes, rework, and confusion. Less than ten seconds of summary goes a long way.

Discipline and Motivation

A foreman always ends up dealing with employees who are having personal and work problems. Money problems. Relationship problems. Drug and alcohol problems. Performance problems. Attendance problems. Attitude problems. If you lead long enough, you will experience them all. And though it is often tempting, you just can't fire everyone with a problem.

How do you know when to cut slack and when to crack the whip? It's a judgment call every time. Have you ever been let off the hook by a cop who could have given you a ticket? Most everyone has at least once. He is tackling the same situation you will face on every jobsite: How do you deal with people who are not handling things the way you want them to?

Teaching, Coaching, and Discipline for Accountability

Here are some questions that should help guide your judgment in exercising flexibility on performance and discipline:

- Can you see light at the end of the tunnel for the problem and the person?
- Is the lack of disciplinary action highly visible to others, thus setting a bad example and undermining respect for you?
- If you make any exception for this person, what will others expect as a result?
- Are you cutting slack only because this person is a friend or family member?
- Are you violating company policies or values by being flexible?

All of these constitute "gray areas." But asking these questions to help process a smart decision will give you a foundation for decisive action.

FIVE MINUTE LESSON

Effectively Disciplining an Employee

This is not something you can do every day, but the situation might crop up a few times per year. When it does, be ready for it by taking the steps outlined below.

Many foremen fail to discipline someone properly at the right time. Oftentimes it's because they don't want to be the bad guy or because they simply don't know how. As a result, they let things slide. Ignoring the issue tells the employee that his behavior is O.K.

Today is the discipline action day.

Do This:

- Clearly identify the behavior that the employee has engaged in that warrants discipline.
- Determine the level of discipline necessary. This may include consulting others up the chain of command.
- Actions may include a verbal warning, a written warning, suspension, or firing.
- Make sure you are in compliance with the company's discipline policies.
- Do not take action if you are too emotional (but don't let it go indefinitely).

Say This:
"I need you to pay attention here. I have spent some time looking into your performance, and there is a serious issue we have to talk about. My facts are as follows: _____ [list the stuff that went down]. As a result, we are going to _____ [explain the disciplinary action]."

- Don't sit around and talk to him about it afterwards.
- Don't try to make it all right.
- Don't listen to any excuses or rationalizations.
- Get a signature on any necessary documentation before you conclude the meeting.

Warnings that Motivate

Sometimes guys need a big wake-up call. This is not about motivating a good performer to become better. This is about helping someone who is failing to save his job because he isn't cutting it. The short version? ***Yo, buddy, your ass is on the line***. Most foremen do a poor job of giving employees warnings. They let it ride while they get angrier and angrier until finally they pull the pin and fire the guy.

Warnings are important. They are a motivational "heads up," and you need to learn how to use them. Here are a few tips to keep in mind:

1. Provide a warning when it is warranted. Don't let things slide a few times, because you're only going to undercut the power of the warning when you finally give it.
2. Provide the warning in a confidential setting.
3. Tell the employee exactly what he is being warned about.
4. State what the consequences are for future performance failure.
5. Set up a timeframe for improvement.
6. Ask if the person understands—not if he agrees.

7. Determine whether you want the warning to be verbal or in writing. Remember that a verbal warning provides no documentation.
8. If the next step is termination, tell him.
9. Ask for a commitment to visibly do better starting the next day. Tell him not to let you down.

This is often a last-chance motivational meeting. They have to know it. "Yo, buddy…"

FIVE MINUTE LESSON

Effectively Counseling an Employee

How often do the guys bring their personal stuff to you? Based on discussions I have had with foremen, it happens on a fairly regular basis. Foremen are often more than just a boss to their crew. At various times, they also serve as banker, confessor, psychologist, or bail bondsman. Sometimes it isn't pretty.

When a guy comes to you, listen carefully and respectfully. If he trusts you enough to bring out his personal side, show him some compassion. On the other hand, if you think it is a set-up for special consideration or an excuse for failing miserably, you have to cut it short.

Today is about how to handle your employees when they come to you with personal problems or situations. There are a few ground rules you have to keep in mind:
- Don't buy a lame excuse.
- Don't lend money.
- Don't let sympathy or emotion cloud your rational judgment.
- Don't get involved in any family situation.
- If the problem is related to drugs or alcohol, encourage them to seek help. They can't be on the job if they pose a hazard to themselves or others.

Always tell the person to do the right thing—not according to you, but according to himself. Encourage him to deal with things directly. Stress that delaying a painful decision or action usually makes things more complicated.

Say This/Do This:
"Look, I have been through some tough times myself. I know it is not easy." Then listen. Then say, "I understand how you must feel."

Don't give any impression that you are going to fix anything. Decide what you are willing to do at work to help them overcome their issues, but remember: You must always treat everyone the same, regardless of what's going on in their personal lives.

Deal with Employees in **Private**

When you have to criticize any employee for something he did—or didn't do—try to do it in a private setting. You don't need to humiliate him in public. Now, don't get me wrong: There are certain times when a public ass-chewing is the right approach to take, but not regularly.

Over the long term, embarrassing someone usually doesn't lead to an improvement in his performance; it leads to less risk-taking and more cover-your-ass thinking.

No one wants to get called out in front of others. No one is usually more motivated after being made to look like an ass in front of others. If you warn someone in a private setting and he still doesn't get it, or doesn't want to get it, then get rid of him.

Leveraging **Failure**

To motivate others, you need to learn to accept failure. It builds scar tissue. It toughens the mind and spirit. It is a fact of every jobsite that sooner or later, someone (or something) will screw up.

BUT...you should recognize that this kind of failure can still have value.

Failure tells you a lot about yourself and the guys on your crew. Some individuals and teams don't deal well with failure. They, well, *fail* to use it as a platform for additional motivation and system improvement. Failure is awesome. It is a whack on the side of the head. Here are ways failure can help make you a better foreman and motivate the people you lead:

1. **Failure as a learning event.** Use the failure to figure out what went wrong and how to avoid doing it ever again.
2. **Failure as an assessment of risk-taking behavior.** Was the failure a result of an unacceptable risk that someone took? If so, why did he take that risk? Was it a personal decision or one mandated by the contractor or the culture of the work crew?
3. **Failure as a way to test the judgment of your guys.** If the failure was directly caused by one of your guys, this is a good opportunity to have a talk about his decision-making process. What factors went into that choice? How can he make better choices in the future?
4. **Failure as a method of assessing motivation.** Does a failing employee come to you disappointed in himself or with a cover-my-ass attitude and an excuse? How your employees respond to their own screw-ups will tell you an awful lot about their motivation and character. That's important information for any foreman to file away mentally.

People, Decisions, and Carpet Surfing

In order to promote accountability and performance, many times a foreman has to make difficult or unpleasant decisions. The more difficult and unpleasant the decision, the more motivated people can be to just put it off. This is not unusual at all. Most of the time, these decisions have to do with people.

It is not hard to delay important decisions like these. We like to tell ourselves:

- It will (just) work out.
- It will (somehow) get better.
- Time (or something) will take care of it.
- It doesn't matter that much (right now).
- I will get to it (eventually).
- It is too much of a hassle to deal with (even though I keep thinking about it).

None of these are very good excuses for not doing what you have to do. Because most of the time when you are making decisions regarding *people*, time is not your friend. Procrastination ends up causing you more stress and grief. Avoidance just makes it much more painful when you finally have to deal with it.

Teaching, Coaching, and Discipline for Accountability

I have never met one foreman (or a leader in any other business) who does not have at least one people decision he has been delaying for some reason.

Sometimes you just have to yank the Band-Aid off and feel the sting. I want to share with you how to do it.

Be a dog.

If you don't understand the necessity and rewards of prompt action, take a clue from your family dog. For he acts like the Harvard MBA he really is. He is a decision-making wonder. For though he may slobber and woof and wag his tail—he also knows how to Carpet Surf. This is what you, too, must do as a master foreman.

You ever see a dog with some poop stuck on his butt? What does he do when he discovers this poop? He immediately sits his crappy butt down on your Stainmaster carpet and scoots all over until he has gotten the poop off. Smart dog. Good dog. Great decision making.

The dog does not over-think the issue. The dog does not stall and pretend. The dog does not rationalize. He does not put it off for later. Your management genius dog understands the following problems with a delayed decision better than most leaders and foremen:

- Everyone can clearly see it (except you).
- The longer you delay and leave it, the harder it is to finally get off.
- You look stupid with it on there.
- You are not fooling anyone.
- There are going to be uncomfortable or embarrassing moments during the removal, but it will be worth it in the end.
- When it's gone, the dog does not think about it anymore and happily proceeds to licking a favorite body part.

Your dog is a management genius. He is your new role model. Follow his methodology. When you are faced with a people decision that needs to be made—no matter the reason you want to delay it—just Carpet Surf. Get on it. Do not delay. Do it now. Do it happily. Learn from him. Woof.

CHAPTER 6

GOAL SETTING FOR PRODUCTION AND PROFIT

"I've worked too hard and too long to let anything stand in the way of my goals. I will not let my teammates down and I will not let myself down."

—*Mia Hamm*

Goals are essential to life. Without goals, it is hard for individuals and organizations to orient themselves towards the future.

- The goal for today
- The goal for tomorrow
- The goal for this project
- The goals for this year
- The goals for your career.

They all chain together. Goals drive results. Goals make action relevant. Goals are incredibly important on the jobsite.

Why? Goals create a specific and visible measurement. For people who really want to accomplish something, goals are the only way to go. In every sport, the score reflects the ultimate goal of the team. It is kinda the same in life. **Winning needs measurement. Goals push.**

So if all this is true, then how come over 90% of the foremen I work with don't communicate goals to their employees? Is there a difference in performance for the other 10% who do? I think the answer is absolutely for sure; in other words, *yes*.

The very basic leadership concept here is that goals and measurements impact performance. If you use goals and measurements, you are always in a better position to show your employees their progress.

Key Elements for **Setting** Your **Goals**

Here are the key elements to keep in mind when creating goals for your crew:

- Goals must be specific.
- Goals must be measurable.
- Goals must be achievable (not ridiculous, or else they will de-motivate).
- Goals must be relevant to those trying to accomplish them.
- Goals must be timely or time-driven.

All of these elements combined make goals real and tangible. They make the effort of the individual, team, or organization meaningful. Measures such as time, hours, incidents, schedule, and so forth can all be powerful motivators if used properly.

More Goal-Setting Mechanics

You might think that setting goals is a complicated process. In reality, it's not that difficult. I have been writing down and setting goals since I was twelve years old. I think there is something to writing goals down. Somehow it makes them real. Somehow, after it is in ink, it is like ***I have to do it***.

No one taught me goal setting—it just seemed to make sense. Now I consider it one of the most important things I have ever done in my life. Many of my goals were even written down in beat-up notebooks—but eventually checked off later—sometimes years later.

Here are some of the mechanics to keep in mind when setting goals:

- **Use metrics.** Think of goals as a set of directions to get from point A to point B. Have you ever tried to drive somewhere using lousy directions? Bad directions can be incredibly frustrating. The same is true for the direction of the project.

  Your goal must indicate if you have "reached your destination." If you've ever been on a long road trip with your kids, you've heard the phrase "Are we there yet?" a thousand times. When it comes to goals, you need to be able to answer that same question. "This goal will be achieved when I/we accomplish X."

- **Finding the push point.** When you are creating goals, you need to strike the right balance. Goals must be challenging but realistic—they should push you beyond the comfort zone but still exist within the bounds of reality. A goal to lose twenty pounds in ten days is certainly challenging, but it's also unrealistic—unless you chop off your leg.

The easiest way to kill motivation is to set unrealistic and unachievable goals.

FIVE MINUTE LESSON

Setting Production Goals that Work

Every day (or at least once a week) you should communicate production goals to your crew. Don't put people on the jobsite to perform tasks. Get them out there to meet goals. You can use different measures, but you have to make it real and tangible for them.

Set goals for your crew like this:

- **Production vs. the schedule—the percentage of any project completed against the schedule (show it visually if you can)**
- **Total labor hours for the project**
- **Your crew vs. other crews**
- **Footage or units installed vs. time (by day, week, month, or segment of work)**
- **Safety vs. hours worked without accident, injury, or lost time (number of hours since the last incident)**
- **Segments or phases of work completed by day, week, or month**
- **Quality: "call-backs" per month or in a year-to-year comparison.**

After setting goals also make sure that you:
- **Review the goal at the end of each day or week**
- **Give them feedback on their progress**
- **If they exceed the goal, show appreciation.**

When you start out, make sure you set your employees up for initial success. Build on small steps so that goal-setting becomes a regular part of their day, week, or month. Don't be afraid to challenge them, but don't beat them up if they come up just short.

Be Open with Goal **Progress**

Some leaders worry about employees slacking off because they reach the goal that was set. That is why a lot of foremen always tell their guys that the job is behind schedule when in fact it is on track or even ahead of schedule. The guys aren't stupid. They know when foremen tell them the same story over and over that every job is not behind or losing money.

You have to start out with the belief that people *want* to be successful. People *want* to be on a winning team. People *want* to beat their own performance, or their old records, just to see if they can, to see how far they can push themselves.

Be honest and open about goals and your progress towards them. Pump up the team with positive reports. Fired-up achievers want to be winners.

Using **Team** Goals

As a foreman, most of the time it will be up to you to set production goals. When possible, however, get your team involved in setting goals, too. That doesn't mean giving up your responsibility as a foreman and letting them create their own rules; you always have the final say. But getting them in on it makes it their goal, too. Ownership = effort.

The importance is not really in what the crew says but in the fact that you asked them for their thoughts in the first place. It's all about ownership and people being directly involved in the plan from the beginning. You are creating accountability for them to meet their own expectations.

Asking for buy-in from the team when it comes to goals almost always equals increased motivation.

CHAPTER 7

BUILDING TEAMS AND RELATIONSHIPS

"The secret to success is good leadership, and good leadership is all about making the lives of your team members or workers better."

—*Tony Dungy*

A construction crew is a team, and as foreman, you're the glue. Your goal is to make sure that everyone is working together and not simply as a loose collection of individuals who occasionally cooperate in order to complete a task.

But there's only so much you can do to ensure that this happens. At a certain point, it's up to the guys on the team. They have to want to cooperate and support each other. The interaction that they have with each other impacts production, quality, safety, and almost everything else on the job.

Your job as a leader is to *create an environment* that fosters cooperation, connection, and support. No sports team ever won a championship without these three elements. No amount of talent can overcome lack of team spirit and belief in each other.

Trust in You = Team Performance

If they are going to bond, your team has to trust your leadership. If they are going to buy in to each other, they all have to buy in to you first.

Like the dominant Alpha of a wolf pack, the team leader has to live up to team members' expectations. If there is a disconnect, then the team can become unstable or fall apart.

Trustworthy Team Leaders	Untrustworthy Team Leaders
Confident	Insecure (so they overcompensate)
Driven	Egotistical (so it's not about the work outcomes, but them)
Internally motivated	Externally driven (focused on showing
See people as a resource	Always see people as competitors or judge them in comparison to themselves
Balance self-interests with those of employees and the organization	Sometimes put self before organization, and always before employees

You Lead **People** and **Teams**, Not Employees

If you want the best performance from your team, you will treat the individual members as people first and employees second. They will know the difference.

The busier you get and the more pressure you are under, the harder it will be to remember that those working for you are people before they are employees.

FIVE MINUTE LESSON

Identifying Qualities of Team Performance

If you watch any team sports at all, you know there is a huge thing called team chemistry. No matter how good the players are, team chemistry makes all the difference. The kinds of things you work on to improve team chemistry (and performance) include cooperation, mutual support, communication, shared resources, encouragement, competition, and accountability.

Do This:
Today is about focusing on improving team chemistry and the performance that comes with it.

- Focus on one of the key team attributes listed above for five minutes. You can do one each time over a couple of weeks (or months).
- Call a jobsite huddle before the shift.
- Communicate the key teamwork value that you think will make a difference with your crew.
- Don't be embarrassed. You are there to get results. You think a winning sports coach is reluctant to talk to his guys about teamwork?

Say This:

"Today I want you guys to think and act like a team, not just a bunch of guys on the crew. You know that you are supposed to have each other's backs on safety, but that is not all of it. For today I want you to try to _____ _____ [outline the team element you want to see]. The reason is that if you do it, the guy next to you is going to do better and be better. And this job is going to go a lot faster and a lot better. I want to see everyone go all in."

Developing Cooperation and Cohesiveness

The first step in building a strong team is to make sure everyone is on the same page and working from the same playbook. The first step toward motivating your team is to give them a complete and detailed picture of the common objective.

Military teams focus on a mission.

Sports teams focus on the outcome of a game.

We are talking about *alignment*—getting everyone to acknowledge that even though they are very different people who may not always like each other, they are a team, and the team is more important than the individual. Get them to buy in to the fact that the team always comes first.

Ten Qualities of Top Performing Teams

Many foremen may want to build a top-performing team, but they don't know how because they haven't been on that many in their own careers. They came up through the ranks like most of us, being supervised by "old school" types who had little interest in positive teamwork.

This is a problem. If you have not regularly been a part of a high-performing, healthy, and fully functioning team, how can you create one? Simple: by observing other great teams and modeling their approach. It's the way we learn how to do almost any important task.

I have been studying great teams for years. Championship sports teams. Special Forces teams in the military. Business teams and allies. Charities that set the bar for participation and support. You name it. So I'll give you a valuable shortcut to creating your ideal team. Here are the ten qualities your winning team needs to develop:

1. Agree on and pursue visible and challenging goals.
2. Encourage positive communication among members.
3. Develop and maintain positive relationships among members.
4. Solve problems and make decisions rapidly.
5. Successfully manage conflict.
6. Have short but productive meetings.
7. Create clear roles and accountability for all team members.
8. Operate in a productive way, both individually and as a team member.
9. Show effective team leadership.
10. Provide learning opportunities for team members.

FIVE MINUTE LESSON

Promoting Positive Change

A good foreman has to be a good change agent. A lot of guys have the attitude of, "We've always done it that way." It is one based on comfort with the status quo. But it rarely generates more opportunity.

Promoting change is about getting your guys to try different things. This could be operational, tools, technology, procedures, or policies—anything that makes the jobsite simpler and better.

- Any time you hear an employee say, "That's the way we've always done it," shut him down right then and there. Remind him that there is always room for improvement.
- Don't let your guys get confused between suggestions for change (which always has a potential solution) and bitching about what they don't like (which never has a potential solution).

Say This:
"I want to hear ideas for positive changes. We want to be the crew where the best ideas always come from."

Do This:
Write down their ideas to show that it matters and to encourage even more of the same.

Basic Conflict **Management**

Guys on your crew are going to get into conflict with one another on a regular basis. Drama and high-maintenance behaviors impact team dynamics and production. As a foreman, you have several choices about how to react when you see conflict between team members:

- Ignore it (so it will go on until sh** really blows up).
- Tell them to get over it (they won't).
- Separate them (not always possible).
- Get rid of one of them (can hurt production or look like favoritism).
- Get rid of both of them (tempting).
- Engage in managing the conflict (not easy, but good payoff).

Why get into other people's "stuff" in the first place? Because it is important that any conflict be taken care of quickly. You want to nip it in the bud before it has a chance to grow. You know how it is. When people get into a beef, they usually try to recruit other people to take their side. That takes up a lot of time and effort that are totally useless and counterproductive.

When you are attempting to resolve a conflict between people, consider these strategies:

- Examine the root cause, not the behaviors. What is the driving reason beneath it?
- Most conflicts are made up of underlying issues that need to be understood before you can get to resolution. These might include:
  a) Competition for power or status
  b) Worries about job security
  c) Passive-aggressive behavior—people are unable to communicate issues or frustrations, so they express their feelings in negative ways
  d) Insecurity of one or both parties
  e) Poor communication skills
  f) Lack of honesty and integrity.

The point is, you usually can't resolve a conflict by looking at the symptoms. You have to find and deal with the root causes.

FIVE MINUTE LESSON

Resolving Conflicts for Better Teamwork

This is an exercise you might not need tomorrow, but at some point over the next few weeks or months I guarantee it will come in handy. This is about stepping in to handle conflict on your crew. Yes, it sucks. But not doing anything generally sucks more. By using a few simple conflict resolution tactics, you can get things back on track much more quickly.

Do This/Say This:
First, identify the parties in conflict with one another. Get them ready. Tell them you know that a problem exists and that you aren't willing to accept any less than a team effort simply because they cannot get along. Tell them that you want to help them resolve the situation but that, in the end, it's really up to them. Here are the ways to resolve a conflict:

- Ask both parties separately what they want specifically as the final outcome.
- Ask them what they have already done to try to resolve the conflict.
- Ask them if they have tried their hardest to fix it.
- Talk to them about the difference between being liked and being respected.
- Tell them they are both fired unless they start getting along (just kidding, kinda).

CHAPTER 8

MENTORING AND KNOWLEDGE TRANSFER

"Mentoring is a brain to pick, an ear to listen, and a push in the right direction."

—John C. Crosby

If you're like me, you didn't get to where you are in life without someone mentoring you. It is part of your career legacy to pass this on to younger people who are coming up in the business. Mentoring is a very powerful motivational and developmental tool that regularly plays a key role in most of our personal and professional lives.

Unfortunately, mentoring is at risk in our industry. I speak to thousands of leaders every year—contractors, CEOs, union leaders, foremen, and journeymen. I ask them all the same question: "How many of you have had someone mentor you for career success?" Every time, almost 90% of the experienced guys raise their hands.

BUT when I ask the follow-up question, the problem becomes clear:

"How many of you are now taking a personal interest in and mentoring someone in your company or industry?"

Now very few hands go up—probably less than 30%. That response is startling. And a problem for the future of the construction industry.

Ask an older guy why he doesn't mentor, and he'll say, "The kids today don't want to be mentored." Ask those "kids"—the young guys in the industry—and they respond, "The older guys don't want to teach us because they see us as a threat to their jobs." Or, "They think mentoring means yelling at us."

This is crazy. If we want our industry to continue on after we've retired—if we want to leave a legacy we can be proud of, something we can point out to our grandchildren—then we need to get on the mentoring train now. Foremen can and should be the most powerful mentors in the entire construction industry.

Consider it a gift to someone who deserves it. Consider the gifts you were given on your way up.

FIVE MINUTE LESSON

Sharing Your History and Experiences

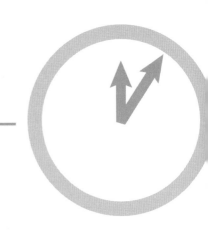

Most foremen have a lot of stories—about projects, people, and everything else under the sun. They also have stories about themselves. These stories can be powerful lessons or just human moments to share with the crew from time to time. Some proud. Some funny. Some tragic. All valuable.

Today's exercise requires you to share any of the following experiences at the right time, in the right place, with the right person:

- When you first started in the business
- The best job you were ever on and why it was so good
- The best crew you were ever on and why it was so good
- Your mentoring story (who was your mentor and what did he teach you?)
- Funny stories where the joke ended up on you. Many times, this is one of the key ways for you to humanize yourself.
- Your biggest mistake and how you dealt with it.

What Does a **Mentor** Do?

A mentor is there to teach, but more importantly, to listen—and then provide support, advice, and good counsel. A mentor is someone who takes a personal interest in you above and beyond a basic relationship. A mentor is someone with whom a real connection of trust, communication, and mutual benefit can be forged.

Mentoring is not about giving someone the skills he needs to take your job. Your fellow workers are not the competition. When you help out the younger guy working next to you, you're helping to strengthen our industry. The better off we all are, the better off you will be personally. That kid may even be supporting your future pension!

You have an incredible amount of experience and wisdom to pass on to someone else. As you go on with your business today, ask yourself what valuable life lessons you have to share that others could profit from hearing.

Mentoring is the last and final contribution a leader gives to his team, his organization, and industry. It is a summary of his experience and advice. I sincerely hope you will take the time to help someone else obtain the rewards and accomplishments that this industry has provided to you.

FIVE MINUTE LESSON

Coaching the Apprentice

Everyone was the rookie at one time or another. Most of the time guys hassled or ignored you. No one loves the new guy. But a little coaching goes a long way. Want a loyal guy who will bust his ass for you? Be the first foreman to coach a rookie in a positive way.

Do This:

- Identify the rookie.
- Watch what he is doing right and wrong.
- Listen to see if other guys are giving him sh**.
- Take him aside at break or at lunch.

Say This:

"Look, I was the rookie a long time ago, too. Here is what I learned: _____. Also, don't let the guys get to you. A lot of people out here know that we have to make sure you younger guys succeed."

Generational Knowledge
Transfer

With many young people coming into the industry, there is a great need for what I call generational knowledge transfer. This is not just mentoring—as in helping someone to succeed. This is the traditional passing down of information that those with the most experience and time served can provide to those on their way up. This includes the tricks of the trade.

It is part sharing, part teaching, part history lesson, and all useful. The obvious payoff is the lessening of the technical and relational learning curve that the new guys have to overcome. The less obvious benefit is that it actually improves the jobsite productivity, quality, and long-term success of the company and industry. Don't make the next generation reinvent the wheel.

This knowledge transfer is really a conscious effort by those who will exit soonest to do something really valuable and important with the lifetime of expertise they have accumulated. A twenty-five-year career can simply disappear without a trace unless there is some legacy created—one that is passed down deliberately and with sincere intent. It is for those who have the knowledge to be willing. It is for those who want and need the knowledge to be worthy.

FIVE MINUTE LESSON

Mentoring Your Next-Gen Talent

Every foreman should be actively mentoring one or two people on his crew or in his company. At all times. No exceptions. This is both an economic and an operational responsibility of a top foreman. But it doesn't stop with you. Everyone at the journeyman level should be involved in mentoring as well.

Today is about taking action on mentoring. Promoting it to all the experienced guys around you.

Do This:

- Bring your guys together. Make sure the most experienced and longest-serving guys are there.
- Ask them if they are involved in mentoring anyone now.
- Tell them that it is important, because these kids are going to be the future of the industry.
- Remind them that these young people will probably be paying their pensions.
- Ask them to take just a little time and share their knowledge and experience.

Say This:
"Someone probably did it for you. Now it is time to do it for someone else. This is not me asking you to be a do-gooder. This is a good way to do business and even ensure your future."

THE FINAL WORD AND BOTTOM LINE

"I'm sure there's a right way and there's a wrong way. The bottom line is you have to do what you think is right."

—*Mike Singletary*

Construction is a rough, challenging, and sometimes brutal business. There is no room for those unwilling or unable in our leadership ranks. This kind of environment breeds a special kind of leader and competitor. But it is important that the rough nature of construction does not cause our leaders to forget the best way to manage the people side of the business.

This takes self-awareness. It takes empathy and compassion. It takes intuition. It takes drive and determination. It takes focus on yourself and others. If you have come this far, you certainly show that you value all of these qualities. As you read the words and applied the lessons in this book, I hope one thing really stuck: **That you really are worth investing in as a person and a leader. Your own importance on the jobsite needs to be recognized—most of all by you.** This importance and new self-identity need to be the foundation for unleashing the full potential of your talent. In giving a little bit of time to the process of self-improvement, you not only own the title "professional" but also have the opportunity to perhaps be a better person.

So now it is about making it work for you. Taking action. So go out and make some money. Go out and inspire that crew. Communicate better than ever. Motivate them until their hair is on fire. Grow our next generation of leaders. Embrace the opportunity. Be who you are.

Rough diamond. Bad ass. Professional.

Acknowledgements

There is not one thing I have accomplished in my entire career that was not influenced by others. There are so many people who have contributed to who I am and what I create that I could never do justice to them all. But I would like to recognize a very influential few.

I would like to thank Gary Andrews, Randy Eppard, Eric Waterman, and Jim Cederna, whose vision and mentoring have kept me on the cutting edge and drinking upstream from the herd.

To David Acord, Cathy Bowman of About Books Inc., and Karen Parry of Black Graphics for their exceptional editorial and design talents. To Jackie Dixon for her remarkable support to me and to our many client organizations.

To my family, and this time especially to my daughter Michaela, who is as tough, smart, and brutally honest as most of the foremen I hope to influence.

And finally, to the almost 300,000 contractors, apprentices, journeymen, foremen, union leaders, construction owners, and training professionals who I have had the unbelievable privilege to serve as a speaker, strategist, or author: my sincere and humble thanks as I keep trying to be one guy making a difference.

About the Author

Mark Breslin is the fourth generation of a construction family. His great-grandfather, grandfather, and step-father were all contractors. Mark started his working career in the field.

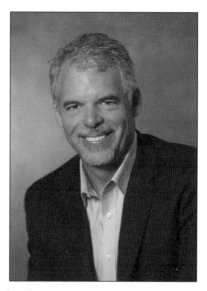

For over twenty-five years he has served as the CEO of United Contractors, one of the largest contractor organizations in the Western U.S. The association represents hundreds of contractors performing billions of dollars in projects annually. Mark became the chief executive at age twenty-six.

He is noted as the number one speaker in the nation on construction leadership, strategy, and labor-management relations. He is also the author of five best-selling books focused on creating positive change in the industry. As a strategist and speaker he has addressed more than 400,000 business, labor, and construction-owner leaders, including many of the top contracting firms in North America. He also speaks to tens of thousands of field craftsmen and apprentices across the U.S. and Canada annually.

Mark graduated from San Francisco State University with a degree in Industrial Design. He has since taught at both Golden Gate and Sonoma State University. He lives in northern California with his wife, Karen. Real-life passions include expedition and adventure travel. Recent challenges include paddle rafting down the Grand Canyon, trekking to Everest Base Camp and hiking the Inca Trail.

Other titles by Mark Breslin

Alpha Dog
Leading, Managing & Motivating in the Construction Industry

Million Dollar Blue Collar
Managing Your Money for Work & Life Success

Survival of the Fittest
How the Future of Union Construction Depends on Every Journeyman, Every Apprentice and You

---

Training Available for Individuals and Companies

More resources at
www.breslin.biz
or call 925-705-7662

PROFESSIONAL CONSTRUCTION LEADER

This educational series delivers leadership lessons to your field leaders over the course of a year, with Mark Breslin as your Coach.

- An On-Demand library of video coaching lessons accessible 24/7
- All videos 2 to 3 minutes— brief but powerful
- Follow up discussion questions to reinforce lessons
- Short, practical and ready to put into action
- Speaks the jobsite language
- Videos include English/Spanish subtitles as user options

How To Make Great Decisions With Your Time

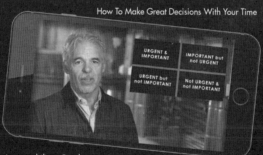

Empowerment + Accountability = Results

- People do their best work when they're empowered
- Empowerment needs accountability
- Accountability has to be measurable
- Empowerment plus Accountability can be a learning opportunity

Subscribe | Advance | Succeed
925-705-7662
breslin.biz/PCL

Breslin STRATEGIES INC.